The Story of Active and In Touch Frome 2011-2021

A Community's Response to Loneliness

John Samways

authorHOUSE®

AuthorHouse™ UK
1663 Liberty Drive
Bloomington, IN 47403 USA
www.authorhouse.co.uk
Phone: UK TFN: 0800 0148641 (Toll Free inside the UK)
      UK Local: (02) 0369 56322 (+44 20 3695 6322 from outside the UK)

Published by AuthorHouse 11/11/2021

ISBN: 978-1-6655-9376-2 (sc)
ISBN: 978-1-6655-9375-5 (hc)
ISBN: 978-1-6655-9374-8 (e)

Print information available on the last page.

This book is printed on acid-free paper.

To Poppy, Dylan, Harry, Phoebe ….. and Frome
You understand – we are called to make a world of difference

CONTENTS

FOREWORD

As a culture, we are obsessed with the latest hot topic, the novelty of today's headlines, and what's trending on Twitter. In short, we are obsessed with things that are new and things that are in the news. This lively little book challenges us to consider a longer span, as it confronts us with one of humanity's oldest and most damaging disorders: loneliness. To judge by one well-known story of human origins, loneliness is the oldest problem of them all, for there we learn that Eve was created because 'it is not good for the man to be alone'.

As this book is published, the people of the UK are starting to come out of the shadow of Covid-19. Over the period of the pandemic, we have been forced to learn the perverse lesson that 'it is not good for humans to be with others'. The tragedy of our fractured modern society is that we were living by that maxim long before Covid-19 hit. We keep in touch by texts, emails, and messages of every sort, but 'message' means a sent thing, when what we all need is to go in person to meet and to be met. I wish every reader could meet the author of this book in person. John Samways is infectious in every good way. He has been a friend for many years, and I can attest to the fact that the enthusiasm and passion in these pages is nothing new, but here, he has helped us to see an old problem in a new way.

Frome is a unique place full of independent stores and independent people. The great vision of Active and In Touch (A&IT) has been to see the deep networks of mutual dependence that make such independence possible. The great work of Active and In Touch has been to make a new network to catch people who might have otherwise fallen out of sight. As accident and emergency (A&E) saves lives by dealing with the acute problems of the moment, so A&IT rescues lives day after day by dealing with the chronic problems of loneliness and isolation. What a great phrase that is: 'in touch'. It's about hands-on engagement and getting a grip. This is in every sense a *hand* book. It is more than a record of the first ten years in the life of a local charity. It is a manifesto for the future of us all.

Professor Gary Watt
University of Warwick
Summer 2021

PREFACE

The year 2020 will be remembered for many things, not the least of which is the increase of our range and use of vocabulary—and I don't just mean expletives! I'll never forget receiving an email (October 2020) with the opening words: 'I'm going cycling along the coast in Dorset this weekend. I'm "bubbling" with a friend.' I paused and smiled as I pondered what that might involve. Social distancing, lockdown, bubble (used as both noun and verb), shielding, wearing masks—all these words and phrases became part of our daily dialogue, not to mention *that* word, namely, Covid.

The word Covid was created from **coronavirus disease**, first identified in 2019, and was purposely chosen by the World Health

Organization and United Nations in an attempt to end the stigmatising impact of diseases being named after places or animals. Spanish flu, a worldwide epidemic 100 years ago that killed more than 40 million people, was subsequently referred to in the press with racist undertones. Likewise, MERS (**M**iddle **E**astern **R**espiratory **S**yndrome) has led to survivors being labelled 'dirty', while references to swine flu and bird flu have led to the wide-scale slaughter of animals.

Ebola has had a devastating impact in West Africa in recent decades and was first identified in the Congo, in a village called Yambuka. When scientists in the United States studied the disease, they selected a name by choosing a nearby river to reduce any stigma for the village. Looking up at a map on the wall in the research laboratory, the closest river appeared to be the Ebola. Alas, the map was inaccurate, and the Ebola River is not the nearest to the village, but the decision had been made. Subsequently, the basin of the river has been permanently tainted and brought into disrepute. Words matter.

This linguistic journey is not confined to 2020. During an interview on television on Sunday 3 January 2021, Sir Mark Walport, a member of SAGE (Scientific Advisory Group for Emergencies) and current chief executive of UK Research and Innovation, stated, 'A "Retrospectoscope" is an infinitely powerful instrument', accompanying these words with a twinkle in his eye. Retrospectoscope was a new word to me (one to remember for future Scrabble contests) and Sir Mark was referring to a hypothetical instrument that allows diagnostic management decisions to be made with medical hindsight. He stated, 'It is an instrument handled, frequently with loud conviction, by those who are wise after the event.' For Sir Mark, the word was handled with humour, and a slight measure of disdain towards his interviewer was evident.

This may appear a very odd way to begin to tell the story of Active and In Touch (A&IT). However, it is only with hindsight (holding a retrospectoscope) that the significance of an idea, shared over coffee one evening with a small group of people, can be fully appreciated. On a Tuesday evening in the spring of 2011, Anna Brindle was sitting on a cushion on the floor of our house in the company of ten others. In the midst of a flowing conversation, she simply said that she wanted to share an idea with us.

Nearly ten years later, I contacted Anna and suggested it might be a good time to write the story of the first decade of A&IT. Anna replied, 'Hi, John. I still cannot believe that it was ten years ago! It's amazing all that time has passed and even more amazing that this whim of an idea has gone from strength to strength!'

The phrase *whim of an idea* neatly sums up the rather low-key, understated nature of Anna's contribution to that evening's discussion. In response, everyone in the room immediately thought this was an idea worth pursuing—as long as Anna took responsibility and did much of the work! The following decade progressively revealed much evidence that this idea planted in Anna's heart was deeply significant. On reflection, the idea was truly prophetic, to a degree beyond anyone's imagination, including Anna's.

What was this whim of an idea occupying Anna's heart? To seek to combat loneliness and isolation in the local community.

It is so easy for beginnings to be forgotten and to overlook the context in which an idea is planted. Yet, every stage of growth in life carries its own significance. The tenth anniversary of A&IT is an appropriate moment to pick up our retrospectoscope and look back to the past, to recall the beginnings and the subsequent compelling and still unfolding journey to the present.

Moments of pure serendipity and wonder have been coupled with episodes of deep uncertainty and fragility. Each year has brought its own surprises, joys, new faces, and inevitable challenges. Every step has served to nurture, amongst those involved, a growing sense of encouragement and purpose without ever quite knowing what lies around the corner.

Invariably, such journeys, whatever their joys, are accompanied by an uncomfortable sense of being taken beyond ourselves. We awaken to the truth that we are not in control. It is that same sense which has increasingly gripped humanity—personally, collectively, locally, nationally, and globally—from early 2020. This continues as we journey through 2021, the year which marks the tenth anniversary of A&IT.

It seems to be the appropriate moment to take the next step—to share the story.

However, before we plunge into this particular story, it is important to acknowledge that *every* story is inevitably embedded in a bigger story, a wider context. Each story needs to be understood in its context.

A&IT was birthed in Frome, Somerset, and sought to address the issues of loneliness and isolation in the community. Although focussed upon the local community, the story of Frome is one we all inhabit, a story that relates to our daily lives. It is a story about working collectively with others to refashion the fabric of the community for the greater good. It is a story that embraces hope, shares some dicey moments, and continues to unfold.

CHAPTER 1

'Once Upon a Time'

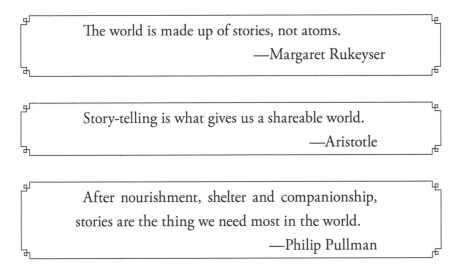

> The world is made up of stories, not atoms.
> —Margaret Rukeyser

> Story-telling is what gives us a shareable world.
> —Aristotle

> After nourishment, shelter and companionship,
> stories are the thing we need most in the world.
> —Philip Pullman

Stories are important. At every life stage, we are in search of a narrative, a story, because stories help us get a handle on life and find order out of chaos. The stories we live by fundamentally shape our lives; they are not childish things to be put away as we grow up.

Albert Einstein (1879–1955) was a German physicist renowned for his intellectual achievements. After he developed the theory of relativity, his name became synonymous with genius. Notwithstanding his intellectual prowess, Einstein loved stories—fairy tales, in particular— and is reputed to have said: 'If you want your children to be intelligent, read them fairy tales. If you want them to be more intelligent, read them more fairy tales!'

For Einstein, the true sign of intelligence was not knowledge but imagination. He believed imagination was more important than knowledge and proclaimed, 'Imagination is more important than knowledge. Knowledge is limited. Imagination encircles the world.' It is fascinating that the story of A&IT emerged not from knowledge but from a whim of an idea, from the realm of Anna Brindle's imagination.

Storytelling has a long and honourable history that predates writing and has played a foundational role in human progress from prehistoric times. The earliest stories were expressed primarily through gestures and artwork, evidence for which has been discovered in Asia, Australasia, the Americas, Africa, and Europe; the oldest cave paintings date back over thirty thousand years. The purpose of these paintings was to help people remember and pass on stories through the generations—stories most commonly told orally. With the emergence of the printing press and, recently, the multitude of opportunities established through the Internet and modern technology, the significance of the oral tradition can all too easily be overlooked. Nonetheless, it continues to play an important role: 'If the whole truth is told, oral tradition stands out as the single most dominant communicative technology of our species as both a historical fact and, in many areas still, a contemporary reality.'[i] It is important that we continue to share our stories.

One of the many ways in which Frome has been blessed has been through the creation of Home in Frome, a community group established through the vision and energy of Jacqueline Peverley. In 2012, the group published a wonderfully engaging book entitled *Working Memories: Frome Workers Tell Their Stories*. [2] Edited by John Payne, the book contains a collection of stories and images gathered through recording people's memories and beautifully illustrates the

2

deep, ongoing significance of the oral tradition. It is a tradition most of us like to continue, whether by leaning on a bar and sharing a pint, chatting over a cup of coffee in one of the many cafés with which Frome and the wider community are blessed, or by simply talking over the garden fence. Sharing stories (not mere gossip) is a precious gift which has been, sadly, temporarily stifled through the impact of lockdown.

Neurological studies have revealed that our brains are wired to understand, remember, and tell stories, which remain central to human communication. From our earliest days, storytelling has had a foundational role in learning, education, and progress. Most likely, one of the first sentences we framed as we began to master the art of speaking was 'Please tell me a story.' ('Please' often omitted!)

Stories are universal and can bridge cultural and generational divides; stories are meeting places—in the neighbourhood, on the touchline, in the pub or café, on the bus, or in the home. By their very nature, stories require us to listen to one another, which can, in turn, lead us to value interconnectedness. Stories can cultivate respect, humility, and sharing. Stories can collapse time and weave the past and an imagined future into the present. They can weave together seemingly unrelated events, revealing an emerging and engaging coherence. Stories don't merely *in*form; they can also *trans*form. Stories can become doorways to new understandings; they can reshape our education and understanding; they reframe how we see things and can redirect our journey of life.

In short, we are all storytelling and story-hearing creatures. This is how we understand our origins, our identities as individuals and communities, and our futures. Stories are not just narratives of events; they are the wellspring of our values, our identities, and our hopes. All stories are multi-layered and, to understand them, we must put them into a wider context, the 'seedbed' into which the kernel of an idea is planted and within which it will germinate.

It is for this reason that the story of A&IT needs to be heard and understood, not merely on its own terms but in the context of the wider story of Frome, including the Covid-19 pandemic in 2020.

The story of A&IT is not primarily about an individual or even a group of individuals; rather, it is fundamentally about a shared desire to serve one another in the community. It is 'a story not illustrating the example of power but one illustrating the power of example'.[ii] It is a story birthed and earthed in the wider community of Frome, a story which will bring a smile or perhaps a tear and offer new perspectives on how we each might choose to 'grow where we've been planted'.

But, before returning to Anna, the lounge floor, and a whim of an idea—perhaps *the* moment of conception for A&IT—we need to consider in some detail the seedbed into which the idea was planted. To understand this seedbed, we must reflect in some detail upon the history of the story of the community of Frome leading up to 2011.

When you visit any new place, be it local or far afield, it is always helpful to find a vantage point from which you can see the big picture because this perspective provides the context for the particular encounters which lie ahead. When chatting about the story of A&IT with Lucia Chadwick, one of the organisation's key stalwarts, I was surprised to learn that 'when viewed from the air, Frome is truly "heart-shaped"—hence the design of the A&IT logo'.

Admittedly, with the rapid increase of building in recent years, that heart-shaped aerial view of Frome is beginning to lose clear definition. Nonetheless, that image provides a powerful framework for the next chapter of the story as we explore the origins of the 'heart of Frome'.

It is particularly important to recall the national and indeed global societal changes unfolding in the post-war decades, especially from the 1960s. These changes have profoundly shaped our lifestyle and the story by which we live. Understanding them throws light on the unfolding changes in Frome, changes so eloquently expressed in the book *Working Memories.*

[i] John M. Foley, What's in a Sign? In E. Anne Mackay (ed.), *Signs of Orality: The Oral Tradition and Its Influence in the Greek and Roman World* (Leiden, Boston and Koln: Brill, 1988)

[ii] John Payne (ed), *Working Memories: Frome Workers Tell Their Stories (Bath: Millstream Books,* 2012)

[iii] A phrase used by Joe Biden during his inaugural address on 20 January 2021

CHAPTER 2

The Seedbed for Active and In Touch: An Overview of the Unfolding Story of the Community of Frome

Part 1: The Big Picture

> What's past is prologue, what to come / In yours and my discharge.
>
> —Shakespeare *The Tempest*

> We have advanced the technique of living at the expense of the art of living.
>
> —Anonymous

> All change starts with a distant rumble at the grassroots level.
>
> —Tom Coburn

You can never make a second first impression. For several years, I drove through Frome from Keynsham on the way to Hampshire or Dorset, always more consumed with my journey to the destination than with the local communities through which I passed. One day in the early years of the millennium, my wife and I decided to actually visit Frome, to wander around and have a coffee. It is no exaggeration to say that we were immediately hooked.

Stepping out of the car, we encountered a curiosity box full of surprises and colours. We were greeted with engaging architecture and creativity; cobbled streets hosting a range of independent shops, and a winding river over which we wandered, across one of the very few bridges in the UK upon which two-storey shops have been built. J. K. Rowling states, 'A good first impression can work wonders', and that was certainly our experience. Frome fosters a spirit of inquisitiveness, an acceptance of nonconformity and, as the *Oxford Mail* declares, 'When it comes to buzz, most towns should want what Frome is having.'[i] What is the history behind this?

The unfolding story of Frome has deep roots. There is some limited evidence of prehistoric and Roman settlements in the area. Headline attention was drawn to this in 2010 when a metal detectorist dug up the largest hoard of Roman coins discovered in Britain—more than 52,500, dating from the third century AD—which was then aptly named the 'Frome hoard'.

The foundation of a monastery in 685 by St Aldhelm, the abbot of Malmesbury, on the current site of St John's Church on Bath Hill, marked the earliest evidence of Saxon occupation, and the significant role of Frome as a market town, acknowledged in the Doomsday Book of 1086, continues to this day. From the fourteenth to eighteenth centuries, Frome was an internationally acclaimed centre for cloth production. In the mid-1720s, Daniel Defoe recorded that the population exceeded that of Bath and that Frome was 'likely to be one of the greatest and wealthiest inland towns in England'.[ii]

Following a period of fluctuating fortunes, in the nineteenth century, the woollen industry was supplemented by metal foundries, notably the brass foundry and bronze-casting works founded by John Singer in 1851. Its work has been exported around the world, and two notable statues in the UK are those of Boudica, commissioned by Prince Albert and standing by the Houses of Parliament and Westminster Abbey, and the statue of Lady Justice holding a sword and pair of scales above the Old Bailey.

The printing industry also gained a foothold in Frome, largely through Butler and Tanner's printworks established in the mid-nineteenth century, as did the brewing industry. The introduction of gas-lighting in 1831 and the railway in 1850, together with the provision of a piped water supply and sewers towards the end of the nineteenth century, prepared the town as it stepped into the unimagined challenges and opportunities the twentieth century would offer.

Through the opening decades of the twentieth century the population of Frome actually declined but after the Second World War Frome witnessed profound changes, including significant growth in population from 10,000 to the current figure of 27,000. Many of these changes have been recorded by members of the Home Frome group celebrating and recording countless oral histories from local residents who were willing to share their experiences of the unique, changing character of Frome through the course of their lives in the twentieth century. John Payne's *Working Memories: Frome Workers Tell Their Stories*, offers an engaging selection of personal reflections of the way local residents lived, worked and played through the post-war decades, and the book paints a wonderful picture of the significant societal changes taking place.

> 90% of the shops were owned by local people, so all the money spent in the town stayed in the town and circulated in the town all the time.
>
> —Jim White, reflecting on Frome in 1950s

> It used to be all hustle and bustle here on Saturdays. Crowds of people walking up and down, but of course there were no supermarkets ... everything was more or less local.
>
> —Robert Hawker

From the 1950s, the scale and speed of change were unrelenting and it was the *Swinging Sixties* that really set the ball rolling. Coined 'the decade that shook Britain', the 60s launched a transformation of almost every realm of life. Memories of the Beatles and the Rolling Stones, miniskirts, Twiggy, and a growing CND movement quickly conjure up recollections of the unfolding social revolution, largely led by the younger generations who began to question the authority and the power of institutional bodies. In a BBC programme in 2021 a presenter, discussing the Beatles role in the changes in the 60s, commented, 'They turbocharged the idea that life is all about *you*, what *you* think, *your* personal opinion.' Significantly, the presenter added the opinion, 'Looking back, you can see how damaging that was, as well as liberating.' It is well worth pondering that statement as we take a bird's eye view of the changes which continued to impact society in succeeding years.

As the 1960s concluded with the monumental achievement of landing Neil Armstrong and 'Buzz' Aldrin on the moon on 20 July 1969, the buoyancy of two decades of post-war economic growth was about to encounter the many political and social issues which spanned the 'Subversive Seventies'. Of all the post-war periods, the 1970s has received the worst press. Strikes and electricity cuts, the oil crisis and soaring petrol prices, financial crises and growing unemployment, Ted Heath and Arthur Scargill, rubbish piling up in the streets and growing violence in Northern Ireland—each episode generated countless headlines of anger and despair. Yet, despite this unpromising backcloth, the decade brought a whole range of new experiences and choices for ordinary people that could not have been imagined by their parents. The most obvious example is the package holiday abroad, opening up the opportunity for global travel.

In spite of the many crises, the 1970s marked an era of increasing disposable income, growing homeownership, and expanding purchases of toys and fashion items. Remember the space hopper, skateboards, tie-dye shirts, bell-bottoms, and hot pants? With the increase in household goods, less time was spent house-cleaning and cooking (the microwave oven was introduced in 1974), the number of professional working women increased, and the decade ended with Margaret Thatcher walking into 10 Downing Street as the first female prime minister.

Surveying these changes as they unfolded across the world, the US author Tom Wolfe, coined the phrase the 'Me Decade' for the 1970s. Wolfe perceptively detected that the concerns of most people, suddenly presented with a whole new range of choices in the midst of much political and economic uncertainty, shifted their focus from the social issues of the 1960s to more personal concerns regarding individual well-being. Wolfe identified a growing desire not to change the world but to prosper within it. Consumerism was preparing to take centre stage.

It's little wonder that for many, the 1960s and 1970s marked a significant turning point in the story of modern Britain. In particular, it is the period when post-modernism, in its quest for radical, individual freedom, began to shape social and political thinking. Post-modernism fostered an attitude of scepticism towards the role of institutions, a distrust of absolute truth and reason, and the dismissal of the relevance of any 'grand narrative', an all-embracing, unifying theory of life. It marked the acceleration of a quest to establish the 'self' and a growing disillusionment with modern society, leading to its progressive fragmentation as Tom Wolfe had perceived.

Through the roller coaster of the 1980s and 1990s, there were repeated episodes of economic boom and bust. The collapse of industrial Britain, overseas conflicts (the Falklands and Gulf wars), Chernobyl, violence on the football terraces and ongoing terrorism in Northern Ireland meant the underlying trends evident in society in the previous two decades continued to gather pace. Accompanying this was an ever-expanding range of choice coupled with a growth in disposable income, significantly fuelled by a steep rise in borrowing, which increased seven-fold in the 1980s.

In the mid-1980s, the UK had more microwave ovens than the rest of Europe combined; there was a rapid expansion of McDonald's and other 'fast food' outlets; *Black Adder* and *Spitting Image* had their television debut; and Barbie dolls became part of the family, carrying the slogan 'Be who you wanna be'. It is acknowledged these dolls had a deeply significant impact, both positive and negative, upon gender issues, feminism, and the role of women in society, together with the importance of body image and self-esteem.

In the midst of this unfolding scene Margaret Thatcher, prime minister throughout the decade, famously stated in 1986, 'There is no such thing as society: there is a living tapestry of men and women and people.' Her words immediately following this oft-quoted statement are invariably omitted, drawing some misplaced conclusions. The statement continues, 'And no government can do anything except through people and people must look to themselves first. It is our duty to look after ourselves and then also to help look after our neighbours.' The omission reveals ever more clearly the growing place of individualism in society as the decade concluded with a further economic boom.

Stepping into the final decade of the millennium brought Frome face-to-face with profound changes and the UK face-to-face with periods of severe recession. Relocation of the Frome Market to Standerwick, the construction of two out-of-town supermarkets and the closure or relocation of significant employers, including Singers, Cuprinol, Beswicks, and Butler and Tanner, had a deeply negative impact upon the vitality of the town centre.

Meanwhile, instability in the currency markets led eventually to Black Wednesday on 16 September 1992 when the UK withdrew from the European Exchange Rate Mechanism. Whilst this move ultimately paved the way to economic recovery, with both unemployment and inflation falling, a profound loss of confidence in the Conservative Party's handling of the crisis ushered in New Labour in 1997.

Yet, in the course of the social, economic and political instability through the 90s, the Channel Tunnel was opened, and the National Lottery launched; 'Friends' appeared on our television screens; roller blades raced down our streets, and Bridget Jones followed by Harry Potter were introduced into our lives. It is little wonder that for some, the phrase *'Carefree Nineties'* summed up the decade which poet and critic Tom Paulin tellingly described as the *'Me, Me* Decade'. The individualism and growing consumerism emerging in the 1960s and 1970s had become progressively entrenched when the millennium arrived.

The 'noughties' will be particularly remembered for two events that had far-reaching effects on a global scale. The first date, changing everything, was 11 September 2001 (9/11) launching the spectre of global terrorism and the oft-used phrase 'War on Terror'. It cast a long shadow.

The second major global event was the Great Recession in 2008-2009, regarded as by far the worst of the four post-war recessions and raising the fear of austerity for many years. As the pace of globalisation progressively quickened through the decade, the debate began to seriously heat up regarding the threat and implications of climate change, coupled with a growing awareness of environmental neglect and rising household debt. All this was unfolding amidst a landscape of rapid, constant innovation in what is coined the *Decade of Technology*. At the heart of all these changes, the emergence of one small word, aided and abetted by an ever-expanding dexterous technology, sums up the growing preoccupation in the heart of Western civilisation. The word is 'selfie'.

Selfie apparently first appeared on an internet forum in Australia in 2002. A young man attached a photo and wrote online, 'Um, drunk at a mate's 21st, I tripped over and landed lip first (with front teeth a very close second) on a set of steps. I had a hole 1 cm long through my bottom lip. Sorry about the focus, it was a *selfie*.'

Subsequent years saw the development of 'smart' technology (based on the idea that your appliances do your thinking for you), the launch of Facebook in 2004, YouTube in 2005, Me Registry in 2006 (offered worldwide in 2008), and Twitter in 2007. The 'tyranny of information' was well and truly unleashed, and the Me domain became the fastest-selling online domain in 2010; by 2016, it had reached over 1 million domain registrations.

The word 'selfie' increasingly became part of the daily vocabulary and won the coveted 'Oxford Dictionaries Word of the Year' accolade for 2013. According to research by Oxford University Press, the use of the word selfie had increased by 17,000 per cent in the course of that year and was officially entered into the Oxford Dictionary in July 2014. The winner of the Word of the Year is judged to reflect the ethos, mood, or preoccupations of that particular year *and* to have lasting potential as a word of cultural significance. There can be little doubt that 'selfie' has justified its accolade.

What has all of this got to do with the story of 'Active and In Touch'?

Pause for thought and consider the following. What has been the cultural significance of the economic, political, and social changes in these recent decades, which have been briefly reviewed here?

'These changes, nation-wide and global in scope, have effected a profound affect upon the wider local community in Frome and upon each one of us personally', as John Payne writes in *Working Memories*,

> The community has grown and changed … in so many ways. The Frome where large-scale enterprise … was located right in the heart of the town has become the Frome of smaller-scale employers, self-employed workers and commuters. The town where everyone knew everyone else (and their business) has been replaced with a more private life-style. The impersonal relationship with the supermarket has replaced many, though happily not all, face-to-face encounters across a shop counter. [3]

The closing decades of the twentieth century and the opening years of the new millennium realised a growing personal income for many. This nurtured an unquenchable thirst for consumption in response to the ever-expanding range of choices arrayed. It is truly ironical that this reality, coupled with an entrenched radical and rampant individualism and an all-embracing technological revolution, served to lead society, dazzled by the apparent riches within reach, to the Great Recession in 2007-2009 and the prospect of enduring austerity. A supreme irony!

In the subsequent decade, leading up to the arrival of Covid-19, social scientists reflected on the impact of the Great Recession and became united in their conviction that society is seriously flawed despite all the advances that have been made. In summary, we have 'advanced the technique of living at the expense of the art of living' and the consequences are far-reaching.

Decades of globalisation, the term that has been given to a range of economic, technological, cultural, social and political forces and processes, have led society to a place where 'social cohesion and engagement are at a historically low ebb' [4] and the implications are profoundly worrying. To coin a phrase, 'we have a problem.'

This familiar phrase relates to one of the most historic and horrifying moments in aerospace history. The Apollo 13 story in 1970 recounts a crisis, which in turn leads into a story of remarkably calm and resourceful teamwork and problem-solving in response. It is a story laced with many heart-stopping, gripping moments, ongoing uncertainties, and overriding tension, which concludes in triumph.

Bearing in mind the crisis arising from the 2008 Great Recession and the spectre and potential implications of austerity in the coming decade, it was a most timely moment to announce, 'Society, we have a problem.'

Alas, the uncomfortable truth is that recognition and acknowledgement of the impact of the powerful trends, forces, and formulas driving social and economic conditions can leave all of us feeling rather helpless. It is as if we are being swept along like autumn leaves. Invariably it is all too tempting to 'go with the flow', to turn a blind eye to the problems before us. We seek justification of our inaction with the thought, 'What difference can I make anyway?' In a telling statement, Professor Peter Cappelli of the University of Pennsylvania commented in 2018, 'What we *could* have taken away from the financial crisis was the resolve to take steps so that it would not happen again. *But it's easier to ignore that, so we are.'*

But not here in Frome!

Part 2: Made Differently

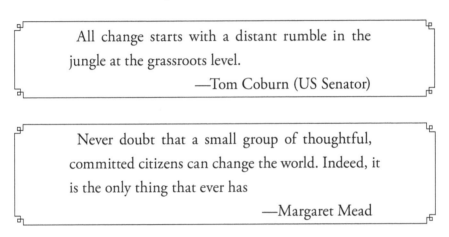

> All change starts with a distant rumble in the jungle at the grassroots level.
>
> —Tom Coburn (US Senator)

> Never doubt that a small group of thoughtful, committed citizens can change the world. Indeed, it is the only thing that ever has
>
> —Margaret Mead

John Payne, the editor of *Working Memories,* concludes the book with the following words: 'Frome is an unusual and very special town. It is particularly fortunate—having a commitment to keeping alive the town's tradition of fiercely-guarded independence.' One of the safest ways of keeping alive a fiercely guarded sense of independence is to acknowledge the important role that rumbles in the jungle can play.

Whilst we in the Western world were being swept along by all the changes being rung through the post-war years, the opening decade of the new millennium experienced a number of rumbles in the jungle in the local community of Frome. These sparked a number of independent initiatives which shared a common desire to 'do things differently'.

Keith Harrison-Broninski recounts in his recently published book *Supercommunities* that this was kick-started by the introduction of the

Frome Festival in 2000. The festival provides a cultural focal point and has inspired and revitalised creative activities across the community. The subsequent regeneration of the Cheese and Grain facility, by an independent charitable trust, into a thriving community hub hosting a wide range of craft and music festivals, played a key role in building further momentum. So too did the St Catherine's Artisan Market.

Initially established in 2009 to bring increased footfall to the independent shops lining the attractive cobbled street, in 2014 the market was rebranded the Frome Independent Market and now takes over the whole town. On the first Sunday of each month from March to December, a number of roads are closed, and tens of thousands of visitors attend. The market, which sadly had to remain closed during the Covid-19 pandemic, played a significant part in further regenerating the creative 'gene', which has played an integral role in Frome's DNA from the beginning.

In addition to these initiatives was the creation in 2008 of Citizens4Frome, a voluntary group of Frome residents. Working with local government and other community groups, its purpose was to produce, promote, and maintain a Frome Community Plan identifying the aspirations for the town over a twenty-year time span, from 2008 to 2028. An unincorporated association and governed by a constitution, Citizens4Frome represented people of all ages and backgrounds from the Frome community. The group was invited to identify problems they saw and to share ideas and aspirations which would achieve the best for the local community.

The chairman of the group was Charles Wood, and the group presented their initial outline plan to the Town Council in 2009 for further discussion. Significant momentum was generated by the 2011 Localism Act, which gives local communities the power to produce a Neighbourhood Plan and, following further discussion and a public consultation in 2013, the plan was finally presented to Mendip District Council in 2014. This excellent, comprehensive plan continues to play a key role in shaping the ongoing, unfolding story of Frome.

A further and perhaps the most significant 'rumble in the jungle' was the fundamental reconstitution of Frome Town Council at the end of the of the opening decade. In his book *Flatpack Democracy*, Peter Macfadyen sets out, in a highly engaging and breezy style,

> the story of how a bunch of ardently non-political party people went from moaning in a pub to running Frome Town Council in 2011. Officially registered with the Electoral Commission as a minor political party and following an upbeat and unorthodox election campaign, Independents for Frome (IfF), a non-partisan collective, gained control winning ten of the seventeen seats. Subsequent elections in 2015 and 2019 resulted in the IfF winning all seventeen seats. Unhampered by the constraints of party politics, the party has been able to pursue its mission to 'make good things happen in Frome' ... to deliver real projects which make a real difference for real people. [4]

It was in January 2011 that yet another rumble in the jungle at the grassroots level was triggered by a resident born and brought up in Frome ... her name was Anna Brindle. The seedbed into which her whim of an idea was to be planted had been very richly prepared.

[i] Carolyn Griffiths, *'Woad to This' and The Cloth Trade of Frome*. Frome: Frome Society for Local Study (2018), 155.

1. Liz Nicholls, Frome: A Wonderfully Weird Market Town, *Oxford Mail* (6 December 2013).

2. Carolyn Griffiths, *'Woad to This' and the Cloth Trade of Frome* (Frome: Frome Society for Local Study, 2018), p. 155.

3. John Payne (ed.) *Working Memories: Frome Workers Tell Their Stories* (Bath: Millstream Books, 2012), p. 32, 45

4. Keith Harrison-Broninski, *Supercommunities: A Handbook for the 21st Century* (Tampa, FL: Meghan-Kiffer Press, 2021), p. 269f.

5. Peter Macfadyen with Peter Andrews, *Flatpack Democracy 2.0: Power Tools for Reclaiming Local Politics* (Bath: Eco-Logic Books, 2019), p. 11.

These books, written by local authors, offer fascinating insights and rich resources which help to unpack the history and potential significance of the unfolding story of Frome. A further recommendation is: Crysee Morrison, *Frome Unzipped: From Prehistory to Post-Punk* (Gloucester: Hobnob Press, 2018).

CHAPTER 3

The Beginning and Early Years of A&IT 2011–2017

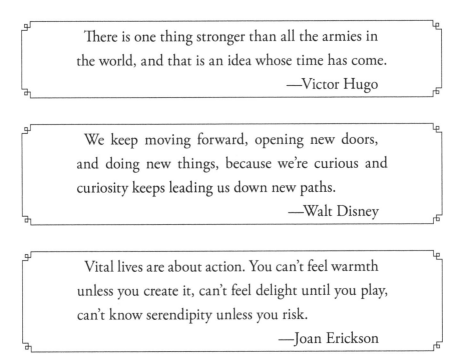

> There is one thing stronger than all the armies in the world, and that is an idea whose time has come.
>
> —Victor Hugo

> We keep moving forward, opening new doors, and doing new things, because we're curious and curiosity keeps leading us down new paths.
>
> —Walt Disney

> Vital lives are about action. You can't feel warmth unless you create it, can't feel delight until you play, can't know serendipity unless you risk.
>
> —Joan Erickson

January 2011 was a memorable month for Anna Brindle. A few months earlier, Anna and her husband, Keith, had attended a Youth Work Conference. Together with all the participants, they had been given a £10 voucher with the challenge to return home and, together with the group they represented (in their case, the youth group at Holy Trinity Church), to come up with an idea of how to multiply the £10. Whichever group turned out to be the most creative and successful would be offered the opportunity for two members to pay a visit, participate in, and experience the work of an inspirational charity in South Africa. *Hands at Work* had been established in 2002 to provide support for the most vulnerable in their communities.

Anna, Keith, and the Holy Trinity Youth Group came up with a novel idea to organise a 'taste and see' ballroom dancing evening. This would be led by a qualified teacher and have the additional attraction of refreshments. Members of the group organised publicity, made canapes, and sold tickets and the evening was a resounding success. In consequence, Anna and Keith's group won the prize, a trip to witness and share in the work of *Hands at Work*.

In January, Anna, together with Charlotte Brown, a member of the youth group, set off for a two-week visit across the equator, and Anna recalls how she and Charlotte flew out with a great sense of anticipation. For Anna, this was heightened by her own quest to find purpose in life. Having recently graduated, she had been somewhat unsettled by her uncertainty as to what route to take in life, the difficulty she had encountered trying to find a job, and her lack of fulfilment working in administration. The flight to Africa proved to be a profoundly significant moment. These questions, residing in Anna's heart and mind, were about to be addressed.

Hands at Work

Hands at Work originated in the north-east of South Africa in Mpumalanga Province. After landing in Johannesburg, Anna and Charlotte took a local flight north to reach the headquarters. Although South Africa is one of the most developed countries in Africa, it has the highest percentage of people living with HIV in the world (18 per cent); coupled with the legacy of the years of Apartheid, this has created a highly dysfunctional and vulnerable society for the poorest people. Recognising the impact this was having upon strained and fragile local communities, *Hands at Work* was established to 'change the way we think about community'. The strap-line, 'All of us need to come together to rebuild the layers of community', underpinned the desire to build resilience and bring living hope to individuals and the wider community.

As soon as they met up with the *Hands at Work* team, Anna and Charlotte were invited to join the workers and the volunteers. Much of their time was spent walking around local communities, chatting to people in the streets and visiting the homes of those identified by the team as orphaned or particularly vulnerable. Invitations were offered to members of these households to join in with small groups of others who were similarly disadvantaged. Each group was taught new skills to enable them to care for others and grow in confidence but also, importantly, to find work and become engaged in the community. It was a simple but effective model. Few resources were required in order for participants to take these first small steps, whilst the shared activities helped to refashion the fabric of the community and build a common purpose.

So fruitful has the project been that it now extends to over forty hubs in eight African countries and has been deemed the 'best-practice model' by a leading international aid programme. One of the *Hands at Work* principles is to invite visitors from abroad to join in with what is happening because 'true partnership impacts you and your community as much as it impacts the African communities.'(www.handsatwork/org) The truth of these words echoes through the story of A&IT.

Anna was immediately struck by the simplicity and clear aims underpinning this work. Also striking was the impact it was having upon *all* those involved, both the volunteers and those with whom they engaged. Each person that Anna and Charlotte met was discovering a growing confidence in engaging with others, and many had been able to replace a disorganised life with a purposeful one. All those involved with *Hands at Work*, vulnerable villagers and volunteers alike, were discovering they themselves could make a difference by offering their own, small contribution into the lives of others.

The two weeks flew by, and Anna and Charlotte returned from Africa with new motivation and much in their hearts and minds to process. Not only had they witnessed an expression of togetherness in the community they had never encountered before but, importantly, had recognised that the charity wasn't simply working *for* the marginalised but *with* them, equipping them with a new-found purpose.

Although the cultural context was radically different from that in Frome, both women intuitively began wondering whether this model would work in the UK. Anna, in particular, was frustrated that nothing she was doing had a similar impact to that produced by the young volunteers she and Charlotte had stayed with in Africa.

Shortly after their return, snow fell in Frome and settled for a few days, causing some disruption. Walking through the snow to the Co-op on the Mount near where she lived, Anna thought, *There must be older people around here who are too scared to go out and who also need some milk. I could collect it, but I don't know they need it, and they don't know I'm here.* As soon as she returned home, clutching her carton of milk, ideas started piling into her head—in particular, the idea of how she might develop a bank of volunteers who could register their willingness to help others and match them up to those who were isolated and alone.

A few days later, Anna was made redundant from her role in administration. She admits it was a job that did not capture her heart, but the news brought understandable despondency and increased a nagging uncertainty about what she was meant to be doing with her life. Then, on the day following notice of her redundancy, Anna spotted an advert in the *Frome Times* for an Active Citizens course about to be run in town. Although she knew nothing about the course, she noticed the training sessions included lunch and that little detail encouraged her to sign up. Reflecting afterwards upon why she *really* wanted to go, Anna realised it was far more than the lunch! Rather, it was the thoughts stimulated by the title 'Active Citizens' which seemed to speak to her desire to find a real purpose for her life. That glance at the *Frome Times* was to have far-reaching consequences, opening up a pathway Anna couldn't have imagined.

Charles Wood, VISTA, and Active Citizens

Anna soon discovered that the Active Citizens course was part of a more comprehensive charitable organisation, VISTA Somerset. VISTA endeavoured to encourage and support local volunteers who wanted to contribute to community life, offering training opportunities and initial funding. Their presence in Frome was instigated by Charles Wood, who had moved with his wife Jane to Frome in 1997, a few years before he was due to retire. Having lived a peripatetic life serving in the RAF, moving from base to base every few years, Charles and Jane were acutely aware of the deprivation arising from the absence of close relationships in the broader community beyond their immediate colleagues in the RAF. With retirement approaching, they wanted to rectify this in their next season of life and set out to become fully engaged with all the Frome community had to offer. Neither Charles nor Jane ever departed from this commitment; even a diagnosis revealing Charles had cancer did little to deflect their resolution to serve the wider community.

One of Charles' early decisions was to join the Somerset Market

Towns Forum, which promotes and supports community-based action to revitalise our towns. Formed in 2003, the forum brings together a network of representatives of market towns and larger villages across Somerset to share issues of common concern and help in the economic, social, and environmental regeneration of local communities. Members of the Forum report back to their local councils, and it was Charles who encouraged Frome Town Council to invite VISTA to deliver a course entitled Active Citizens for the local community. Having trained as an engineer and spent all of his working life serving in the RAF, in later years at a senior organisational level with NATO, Charles was not only a highly successful organiser but also a man who enjoyed working with others. As well as persuading the town council to set up the Active Citizens course in Frome, he signed up for the course himself.

During one of the course sessions, group members were each asked to 'pitch an idea'. Most of those on the course talked about serious long-term projects with which they were already involved, but Anna took another route. Whilst acknowledging that she invariably had a number of ideas floating around which 'usually didn't go any further', she felt prompted to mention this whim arising from her recent trip to South Africa, an idea which wouldn't go away. At the end of the session, one of the course leaders wanted to hear more and, before long, VISTA got back in touch to say there was funding available for a pilot project aimed at helping isolated older people in Somerset. They thought Anna's idea might fit into this and encouraged her to pitch for it. She dutifully followed this up and received funding for a pilot project spanning twelve weeks beginning in the autumn of 2011.

Anna reflects,

> From this moment I started making lots of connections,
> meeting and speaking with everyone I knew who

engaged with the local community—volunteers who ran social groups for older people, mental health workers and Age UK and local church leaders, including Graham Owen at Trinity Church who was very supportive. I've actually always found it difficult making phone calls and networking but once I'd overcome this it was wonderful to hear what others were up to and helpful to discover the gaps. In addition, I started to gather people who showed an interest in volunteering and began speaking to those leading Duke of Edinburgh's Award schemes and similar ventures.

From the outset I had a small but committed group with whom I could try out my ideas. Key members were Dave Revell from church, Charles Wood from Active Citizens, and Clare Scholefield, a good friend who was applying to train to do social work. Things progressed in a rather ad hoc way—volunteers stepped forward and leaflets were distributed randomly around the community. From these beginnings, a list emerged of local residents who would welcome a visit and a chat.

The fundamental idea was simple. It was to watch out for people feeling isolated and lonely, to discover their interests and then to endeavour to match them with someone with similar interests. On one occasion a man called Clive, who had casually picked up a leaflet in the library, turned up at a meeting and expressed his love for walking. There happened to be a prospective volunteer at the meeting who wanted to get fit and was only too delighted to walk with him. They both found enduring friendship together and, ten years later, Clive continues to be one of the first members of A&IT to make an appearance at any gathering.

On another occasion, an elderly gentleman was visited by Anna together with an ardent volunteer, none other than Charles Wood. As the visit was coming to an end, the gentleman added, 'This is the first time a man has been inside my house for ten years!' For Charles and Anna, as well as the gentleman himself, it was a deeply significant moment and it has served as a constant reminder that it is so important to have both male and female volunteers for both have key roles to play.

Lucia

As momentum began to grow, it was in October 2011 that Lucia Chadwick joined the fledgling A&IT. Recalling the moment, she reflects,

> I was a full-time mum at the time, having parked my career in PR and Internal Communications in 2007 when the children were born. Living in Rode and deeply embedded in the wider community of Frome, I had recently come to faith and had just completed the Alpha course. I was now looking for something I could do within the local community that might make a difference. One afternoon, feeling rather unsettled, I sat down and prayed very earnestly for guidance. I so wanted my faith to have purpose, if I was going to talk the talk I wanted to walk the walk.
>
> That very evening my friend Mirjam happened to call me to say that Anna Brindle had started a new project, designed to help isolated and lonely people in the community, and was looking for volunteers. I was

so excited by this and knew immediately, in a bone-deep way, that I wanted to be involved in any way I could. I was unaware that my next-door neighbour, Lizzie, had been along to the youth group meeting in Norton St Philip on the same evening and had also heard about Anna's ideas. She wondered if I would be interested and phoned me the next morning. There was a deep feeling that perhaps this was meant to be.

Lucia phoned Anna the following day and was invited along to the next meeting. On arrival, full of expectancy, Lucia recalls,

> The moment I pitched up I immediately discovered a small group of lovely, engaging, dedicated people who had caught the vision and were eager to work with the variety of opportunities arising and the contacts being made. It was clear that Anna was uncovering a huge need for connection in the community and that whilst loneliness was rarely mentioned in local or national news, it was a growing reality in our midst.

VISTA soon recognised the twelve-week pilot project was having an impact and serving a real need in the community. They offered to continue to steer the project, working out of a tiny, windowless office at the bottom of Weymouth Road, and one of their members, Sara Iles, was appointed to oversee the project. Anna was funded for a few hours each week to continue to develop connections with the local community.

In the spring of 2012, Sara moved to another role in VISTA and was succeeded by Tina Herbert. At this stage, Anna and her family were preparing to leave Frome as her husband, Keith, was about to start training for ordination at Trinity College Bristol. To ensure Anna's role was sustained, VISTA appointed one of their team, Julia D'Allen, to replace her.

By this time, Lucia was by now well embedded in A&IT, and it was not long before VISTA recognised that she was just the right person to succeed Anna and would do an excellent job of managing the service and co-ordinating the volunteers.

At this stage, A&IT had two key priorities:

1. To discover the lonely and isolated, befriend them, and discover their interests.
2. To recruit volunteers with similar interests to establish a continuing, mutually beneficial connection.

It was a workable plan that was potentially accessible for each and every member of the community, spanning the generations. It is this formula that remains at the heart of A&IT and which is serving to embrace a diverse and growing group of local residents who are mutually supportive.

In the course of these early days it was recognised that, in order to get our name known, one priority was to create an A&IT logo. A logo is important because it gives an important first impression, can help tell the story of the group it represents, and can establish an emotional connection with the community. VISTA recognised this and provided the necessary funds.

Lucia had been intrigued some years before by the discovery that if you look down on Frome from a helicopter, you can see the outline of the town is heart-shaped. The significance of that image reinforced the A&IT conviction that the 'heart of the matter is the matter of the heart'.

The heart-shaped image and the name of Frome are highlighted in a different colour on the tenth-anniversary plaques to serve as a reminder that the work of A&IT seeks to embrace the whole wider community of Frome. Quite simply, whatever our background or age, we all have a potential part to play in helping to build a cohesive community from which we *all* benefit. A&IT has evolved from the grassroots of the community and is primarily motivated by the heart-shaped values of love and kindness. The logo expresses this belief.

The Bridge Café

The value of creating small groups was soon recognised as an important step to take. Such groups serve to enrich and widen the A&IT network. They function as a 'gathering place' which supports those taking steps to regain their confidence, following a period of isolation, without being overwhelming. One of the first initiatives involved setting up two small groups, the Widow/Widowers Support Group at the George Hotel in the centre of town and the Active Tuesday group at the Bridge Café on Selwood Road.

Established by Holy Trinity Church in 2003 and run by a team of volunteers then led by Tony Perry, the Bridge Cafe offers simple, affordable food, a place to gather and chat, and access to welfare benefits advice two mornings a week. One of its functions is to help in the distribution of food parcels organised by Fair Frome.

One day a visitor turned up, Di Rogers, offering to provide the café with vegetables from her allotment. Di had trained as a stage manager and worked in the theatre for fifteen years before moving on to live events. As both she and her allotment neighbours had surplus supplies, she had quizzed Bob Ashford, chair of trustees for Fair Frome, as to who might be able to make use of them. Bob duly directed her to the Bridge Café and, from then on, Di continued to deliver the vegetables on a regular basis.

One day she asked Tony if he knew of any volunteer group with which she might get involved. As A&IT had only a few months earlier established their Active Tuesday group in the café, Tony introduced Di to Lucia and the timing proved to be highly significant. Lucia recalls,

> With numbers in the Active Tuesday group quickly growing, we were running different workshops each week led by qualified instructors. The range of workshops was huge. It included how to cook a roast dinner for one, singing water bowls from Nepal, pottery, felting, artwork, card-making, and introducing animals and insects from Longleat! Not surprisingly, we were beginning to feel rather overwhelmed.

What compounded the problem was that VISTA felt Lucia was spending too much of her time dealing with workshop development at the Bridge Café and not enough time nurturing other links with the lonely and isolated. It was at that moment that Di called Lucia and asked if she could meet up with the group and also bring a friend along with her, Suzi Mitchell.

Di and Suzi

From the outset Di and Suzi settled quickly, engaging really well with the group. Di reflects,

> I think seeing the difference the group made to each of its members, hearing all the stories of people's lives and just having a good laugh together, was so uplifting. You could go to the Tuesday Group feeling down but you always left with a smile on your face, feeling better about the world.

Like Di, Suzi felt very much at home in the group and witnessed friendships being established amongst a group of people who would have never met without the opportunity offered by the Tuesday group. As it became difficult for Lucia to pick up all of the members, Suzie helped with the transport and became familiar with many of her passengers' stories, gaining a new understanding of how sad some stories are and how easy it is to unwittingly walk by, oblivious to what some people have to cope with.

One member in particular drew Suzi's attention. Joan, in her nineties, was always ready and waiting to be picked up on her doorstep, immaculately dressed with a matching necklace. When Suzi heard Joan's story, she was both amazed and deeply humbled.

Joan

Joan explained how one day, when she was aged four, her mother walked out of their home in Guildford, leaving Joan alone. Joan never saw her again. As her father was at sea with the Merchant Navy, it was a neighbour who found and cared for her, who wrote a letter to her father to explain what had happened. He returned home but could not afford to leave the Merchant Navy, so Joan was dispatched to be brought up in a children's home. In due course, she married and had a son and a daughter before seeking out a child needing a family whom she could adopt.

In later years, Joan had enjoyed socialising over a coffee in town with her many friends but, sadly, they had all died and Joan felt bereft. She was delighted to discover the presence of the Tuesday group and looked forward with anticipation to each gathering. Patient and a good listener, Joan was a hugely supportive and transforming presence in the group. She was especially good at connecting with those who found joining a new set of people difficult and was a true gift to A&IT—and Suzi.

This evident kindness never ceased to flow from Joan. She never bore a grudge or asked for sympathy but, in her closing years, played such a key role in bringing renewed confidence and joy into other people's lives. It was through these early stages that A&IT continued to discover a rhythm of life that met the hopes and needs of both volunteers and members in mutually beneficial ways.

A smaller social group was established at the Bridge Café on Monday mornings. This was limited in size to make it easier for those who were joining the group after an extended period of isolation. Meanwhile, the larger Tuesday group meeting convened at various venues, including the Assembly Rooms, the Corner House and Phoenix House, and a range of further activities was established. These included tea dances, celebrations at Christmas, local visits, for instance to the Walled Garden at Mells, and the occasional trip to Weymouth.

From the outset in 2011, even here in lovely Frome which is full of buzz, it was apparent that the social fabric of the local community contained many disconnected, seemingly random threads. It became clear that the approach of A&IT, albeit on a very small scale, was unveiling and seeking to address a widespread yet hitherto largely unseen societal issue. This task, enabling isolated lives to be woven back into society and refashioning the fabric of the community, remains an ongoing challenge waiting to be addressed by each and every generation.

Such an approach, given Frome's historical links with the woollen industry and its long-standing reputation in the past for weaving, is one deeply rooted in the town's heritage. The story of A&IT is certainly embedded in a bigger story.

A Significant Development

In 2013, Lucia met up with Jenny Hartnoll, a community development officer for Health Connections Mendip, who was fascinated to learn more about the A&IT story. Jenny was convinced that 'it is important to have one foot in primary care, and one foot in the community' and the conversation she shared with Lucia led both of them to recognise the importance of establishing a link with Frome Medical Practice. This brought about a significant step-change for not only A&IT but also the Medical Practice, whose senior GP partner is Helen Kingston.

Helen, a pioneering GP, had recognised the impact that loneliness was having on her patients' physical and mental health and was in the process of establishing the *Compassionate Frome* Project. Funded by government-backed innovation funding, this initiative was the fruit of an ongoing collaboration between Frome Medical Practice and Health Connections Mendip. One of their first moves was to engage Jenny to map local community resources in order to enable the Medical Practice to work with the existing local social network as effectively as possible. Inevitably, this led to Jenny, Helen, and Lucia sharing ideas and practices, which proved to be beneficial and fruitful for all parties.

As A&IT continued to quietly grow and expand its activities, the need for extra staff hours to supplement Lucia's role became very evident. A grant was secured from the Somerset Community Foundation for an additional part-time post to be established. It was a role for which Di was eminently suited as she found such joy in interacting with volunteers and members, visiting and getting to know them a little and discovering their interests. Appointed as co-ordinator for members and volunteers, Di continues to play a key role in 'mixing and matching' members and volunteers, a crucial part of the whole A&IT operation.

Recalling memories of these early years, Lucia is almost overwhelmed at the response of all those involved:

> Our volunteers always amazed me, time and again they would go above and beyond, their care for others was boundless. Some people to whom we were introduced found socialising hard but the love that was shown to them, through listening, patience and small acts of kindness, all framed with a smile, was healing and enriching. Quite simply, lives were changed, and countless stories testify to this.

Memorable Stories

The stories which could be told are countless, but a couple, in particular, reflect upon the far-reaching consequences of pursuing Anna's whim of an idea in 2011. Lucia recounts,

> A lovely story from the early days emerged from the transformation of two very lonely younger people. I visited one in 2013 who always stayed at home with her mother. At her request I continued to visit and, after several months of gentle encouragement, she agreed to pay a visit to the Active Tuesday group.
>
> Around the same time, a young man living a very solitary life was referred to us. He was grieving, as his wife had died two years previously, and he had reached the point when he was beginning to wonder whether life was still worth living. In due course, the unhurried, patient kindness and concern of volunteers drew him also to the Tuesday group, which he regularly attended.

Two years later, to the joy and delight of all, they got married (I went to the wedding, which was a joyous occasion), and they continue to live in the local community.

The second story illustrates what remarkable strides had been made by Lucia and her colleagues in the five years she had overseen A&IT. In 2016, BBC television launched their nationwide *Street Auction* series of programmes. The format was based on collecting items from members of the local community and selling them at an auction. The funds raised would be given to someone who had served the community in a memorable way.

On 21 May 2017, Victoria Park provided the venue and A&IT the story. Lucia recalls,

> We decided to get in touch with the BBC to see if they would hold one of their Street Auctions for Joe Dismore, one of our oldest volunteers at the age of 91 and truly one in a million. He had been sadly widowed when his wife Rosemary died after sixty-one years of marriage but Joe, instead of feeling crushed by the bereavement, wanted to show his thanks for a very happy marriage by helping others. He decided to join A&IT as a volunteer. Always the first to contact us if we had posted a request to volunteers, he had visited one man for nearly five years, stopping only when his own ill health intervened.

Joe had no idea of any details about the event but was excited to hear about the BBC being involved and invited his whole family to come along to Victoria Park and join in the fun. *The Frome Times* posted the following report of a memorable occasion of the pop-up auction, which raised £1,250:

Neighbours in the Vallis Road area donated unwanted and unloved items, which were sold at the pop-up auction hosted by Paul Martin of '*Flog It!*' in Frome's Victoria Park.

Frome charity Active and In Touch had nominated one of their volunteers, 91-year-old Joe Dismore, to receive the proceeds from the auction as a thank you for all his dedication.

Lucia Chadwick from Active and In Touch said, 'Joe has been a volunteer with us for nearly five years and in that time has helped so many people. He'll be 92 next month but he shows no signs of slowing down, in fact he's just signed up to be a volunteer with Frome Community Drivers!

'We are so pleased he was chosen to receive the money raised from the street auction—he will use it for a VIP trip to a London theatre as his greatest passion is going to the theatre.

'Joe was very shocked and gave a wonderful speech to the camera which had us all in tears. He said that he has been volunteering all his life and he very much enjoys giving back to the community.'

Chris Stringer from Frome Town Council said, 'We were delighted that the BBC chose Victoria Park for the Frome edition of *Street Auction* and it was great to work with them and with Active & In Touch on the event. And good weather meant a really busy and lively afternoon in the park, which is just what we like to see.' [1]

Behind the Scenes

Throughout these early years, there was much encouragement as friendships deepened, and new faces continued to appear. Yet there was also an accompanying, underlying sense of fragility about A&IT. For a growing project, financial provision and staff hours continued to be uncomfortably unpredictable and concerning.

VISTA, whose prime role in the county was to initiate local projects, announced in the summer of 2014 that, as a consequence of the impact that austerity was having on the county council funding, they were withdrawing their oversight of the project. Lucia's contract would be terminated at the end of August.

From September, Lucia continued her role but with no funding, no insurance, and no governance. Overseeing the groups in this voluntary capacity was clearly not sustainable. The day arrived when she felt she had to explain to the Active Tuesday group the reality of the situation and the probability that the group would cease to exist.

That day was Remembrance Day. At 11 a.m. the group had settled down in the Bridge Cafe and Lucia was girding herself to break the sad news, acutely aware that it would be devastating for so many. Just before she got up to speak the phone rang and Lucia hesitantly picked it up, somewhat distracted by what lay ahead. To her utter astonishment and unconstrained delight, it was a call from another county-based charity, Somerset You Can Do who were offering to oversee A&IT, rewrite Lucia's contract and provide further support for the project. Wow! The atmosphere in the Bridge Café that Tuesday morning was transformed and, following later discussions with Charles Wood, Lucia and the team prepared for the future.

Although momentarily thrilling, this unforgettable moment served to underline the fragility of A&IT; Charles Wood was strongly encouraging the group to establish charitable status. The purpose behind this was to ensure proper governance and to gain public recognition and trust. This would serve to strengthen grant-funding applications and build greater stability for the future.

Charles had organised high-level meetings for NATO before his retirement. He was the ideal person to take the lead, much to Lucia's delight, and did much of the work to establish A&IT as a Charitable Incorporated Organisation (CIO). This enables all the members to have a voice in decision-making, a principle embedded in Anna and Lucia's hearts and reflected in their leadership of A&IT from the very beginning. In due course, with the encouragement and support of Frome Town Council, A&IT was finally established as a charitable organisation in 2017.

Through these early years, it is clear that the unfolding story of A&IT embraced a series of serendipitous moments. Each paved the way, step by step, for modest plans and new ideas to be developed and established. From the outset, it was as if just the right people and opportunities presented themselves at very timely moments. Much of this important groundwork was accomplished by Anna Brindle, Lucia Chadwick and Charles Wood, assisted by the hard work of Di, colleagues, and volunteers. Everyone worked way beyond their limited hours.

It was this work that prepared A&IT to react to the challenges which were about to arrive on the doorstep.

1. 'BBC Street Auction raises £1,250 for 91-year-old Frome Volunteer', *Frome Times*, 23 May 2017.

CHAPTER 4

Tales of the Unexpected: 2018-2019

> There is nothing permanent except change.
> —Heraclitus

> When we least expect it, life sets us a challenge to test our courage and willingness to change.
> —Paulo Coelho

> Vulnerability is the birthplace of innovation, creativity and change.
> —Brene Brown

In January 2018 the government took its first steps to respond to the Jo Cox Commission on Loneliness report; loneliness is now recognised as one of the greatest public challenges of our time. Prime Minister Theresa May stated: 'Research now shows that loneliness is as damaging to our physical health as smoking and that loss of social contact is increasingly damaging to our humanity.' In July Baroness Barron, the Minister for Civil Society, was appointed to lead work on tackling loneliness, marking a significant move for the government and the nation.

For A&IT too, 2018 marked the beginning of a period of two years when significant adjustments were made as a result of a series of 'tales of the unexpected'. Each episode was unsettling at the time but, with hindsight, each delivered a further sequence of serendipitous moments.

Changes for Lucia

Having nurtured the development of A&IT for over six years, Lucia was increasingly aware that her role had developed her as a person. It is widely acknowledged by sociologists that to serve others and to volunteer brings mutual benefits to both server and recipient and this has been the testimony of those associated with A&IT, not least Lucia.

Volunteering is invariably a win-win situation for all parties, creating what's termed 'social capital'. Social capital arises from the human capacity to consider others, to think and act generously and co-operatively. Impacting both personal relationships and social structures, social capital is generated through personal relationships based on trust, respect, kindness, and reciprocity. It is regarded as the most precious possession of any form of community life and to be a true indication of the wealth of the community.

Wealth is derived from an old English word 'weal', which fundamentally describes two terms we frequently use today, well-being and wellness. True wealth is not the sum of our cash and assets but the relational capital that exists in our families, communities, and society. Wealth creation, understood in these terms, can unleash untold levels of human flourishing and thriving, heralding life in all its fullness. Such wealth can be transformational. This is particularly the case when all the participants, volunteers, members and staff are working alongside one another, mutually building and benefiting from a shared growth in social capital.

It was this reality that Lucia had experienced through leading A&IT

for six years; she herself was being transformed as she led the group. One of her long-standing colleagues Di, reflecting upon Lucia's leadership, comments:

> I think she was made for the job at A&IT. She brought life to the project and her own personality just fitted with what A&IT is all about: empathy, sympathy, kindness and friendship. She always went above and beyond for the members—she rang one member for a year before being able to encourage her to join a group which, years later, she continues to attend.

Lucia added:

> These years showed me and confirmed my love for people of all ages and from widespread backgrounds. This gave me the confidence to explore the role of counselling, something I had yearned for since childhood.

This comment serves as a powerful reminder that A&IT is not an end in itself, not a destination. Rather, its foundational purpose is to enrich the lives of all its participants, enabling them to 'find themselves' and, in so doing, to contribute towards rebuilding the community's social capital. All this was happening at the very time when social scientists were acknowledging that social cohesion had never been lower.

As her hours serving A&IT were limited by the available funding, Lucia began to explore the possibilities of studying in Bristol for a post-graduate Diploma in Counselling. She embarked upon this course in 2015 and received her Diploma in 2017. In the latter half of that year, Lucia began working part-time with *Focus Counselling*, a highly respected group established in Bath in 1999. Balancing time between the role of managing A&IT in Frome and serving as a counsellor with Focus in Bath was a delicate business; both roles were deeply fulfilling and equally demanding.

Before long, Lucia learnt that Focus, in response to the growing demand for its services, wanted to set up regional hubs to enable it to serve communities distanced from Bath, including Frome. Discussions with Frome Town Council and St John's Church ended with an agreement that an office for Focus Counselling would be established in the building occupied by St John's Office in the heart of Frome. Given her close connection with and knowledge of the local community, Lucia was understandably interested in these developments. She discussed the possible implications with colleagues and the trustees of A&IT and, with some trepidation, they supported her interest. She successfully applied for the post of practice manager for the Focus Frome hub and started work in the summer of 2018.

It was agreed that Lucia would continue her role with A&IT as the office hours in both roles were, on paper, manageable. However, as Focus Frome began to be established and A&IT continued to grow, both Lucia and Di became very stretched. This opened the door for Gwen Corbet to join the A&IT staff team for a few hours each week.

Gwen

Much of Gwen's work, alongside Di, addressed the important role of matching volunteers and members. This is such an important element of A&IT's input, and Gwen's gifts are ideally suited to this task.

Growing up in the Netherlands, her family regularly spent their holidays in central southern England. From childhood, Gwen invariably returned from these holidays with a lingering homesickness remaining in her heart for England. She intuitively sensed that one day she would live in an area she held so deeply in her heart.

Knowing from her youth she wanted to help people, Gwen trained to assist adults with learning difficulties, to discern and develop their skillsets, to provide counselling and encouragement, and to build their confidence. A team player at heart, Gwen had been self-employed before coming to England where she settled in a small village a few miles from Frome. One of her near neighbours was none other than Di.

With hours becoming stretched at A&IT, Di wondered whether Gwen would be interested in exercising her gifts, meeting up and matching new members and volunteers. Following an interview, Gwen was delighted to accept the opportunity to work a few hours each week in the office, specifically helping to run the small Monday group, which plays such a key role in the charity. Gwen reflects,

> At every gathering, there is a tangible sense of a growing atmosphere of mutual confidence and well-being. Both are gently generated, week by week, amidst encounters among the volunteers and members.

Meanwhile, Charles Wood was beginning to struggle with the progression of his cancer which had been diagnosed in 2012. From the beginning, Charles had been a campaigning presence for A&IT as a volunteer, a trusted voice in the realm of local politics, chair of trustees and a fount of wisdom. Predictably, his health situation did little to slow him down and he continued to put his heart and soul into every realm of A&IT. Through the final days of his life, lying on his bed in the Royal United Hospital in Bath, he was still shaping plans on his computer.

Julia

A few weeks before his final entry into hospital, one of Charles' last contributions to A&IT was to put an advert into the *Frome Times* to recruit more trustees. A couple of days after publication his phone rang and he arranged to meet up at Black Swan Arts with the caller, Julia di Castiglione. Following a chat over a cup of coffee, Charles invited her along to the next trustees meeting and to wait outside the door until she was invited in. Julia dutifully turned up at the appointed hour and discovered another potential trustee, Jackie Bryant, who was also waiting to be invited in. The date was 17 September 2018.

After a short while, the door opened. Julia and Jackie were beckoned to join the meeting and were about to step into a 'baptism of fire'! They were rather surprised to find Lucia chairing the meeting and no sign of Charles. After introductions had been completed, both Jackie and Julia accepted the unanimous invitation to join the team of Trustees. The news was then shared by the trustees that Charles had died in the RUH. The trustees of A&IT were without a chairman.

Lucia, understandably still in a state of shock, had recognised that it was important that the trustees' meeting was not postponed because a number of pressing issues were on the agenda. As manager of A&IT, she very reluctantly agreed to take up the role of chair for the meeting. Following correct procedure, Lucia asked whom amongst the trustees would be willing to take up the role of chair.

A deafening silence followed, occasionally broken by 'I'm sorry but not me'. One of the trustees recently appointed, Alan Didymus, offered to become vice-chair but declared firmly he would not countenance becoming Chair. Further silence followed before Julia found herself uttering, hesitantly and reluctantly (after all, this was her 'first' contribution to A&IT): 'I suppose I could do it … I've chaired groups before.'

Predictably, these words opened up a conversation between Lucia and the trustees, and it was clear that there was only one of those present who expressed any uncertainty—Julia! Thus, one of Charles' final contributions to A&IT was to play a key role in recruiting his successor as chair, Julia. Lucia continued in the chair for the rest of the meeting, leaving Julia to ponder the implications of the group's unanimous decision.

Julia had moved to Frome in 2006, having spent her professional career in nursing. After training at Great Ormond Street Hospital and progressing to hold senior posts there and subsequently at the Royal Free Hospital, she came to Frome where, until her retirement in 2015, she worked part-time for both Dorothy House Hospice in Bath and St Peter's Hospice in Bristol. Following retirement, Julia set apart the following year to dig her allotment, walk her dog, and ponder how she might continue to serve the local community in her new season of life.

Within a year, having rested well and moved into the heart of Frome, Julia felt that it was time to take the next step. She decided to accept an opportunity that ideally matched her qualifications, namely overseeing patient care in the residential and nursing care homes in Frome. Having settled into this new role, Julia found herself still wanting to engage with the grassroots of the wider local community and, in an idle moment, opened the latest edition of the *Frome Times*. That was the moment Julia's eyes fell upon the advertisement, and it was only a matter of a few weeks before she joined the trustees.

A Big Decision

At the next trustees' meeting in October 2018 it was apparent to everyone, not least Julia, that they were facing an enormous problem. For seven years the work of A&IT, now being richly complemented by the impressive work of the Compassionate Frome Project, had been seeking to address a problem currently acknowledged nationally. Only the previous month the government had appointed the world's first

Minister for Loneliness, Tracey Crouch, and it was recognised that a lack of social cohesion and loneliness was now endemic in communities.

It was at this very moment that Charles' death had left a group of staff and trustees understandably feeling very vulnerable and uncertain.

Charles had worked relentlessly for A&IT to finally accomplish charitable status in April 2017. However, the requirements of the Charity Commission to ensure appropriate governance generated their own pressures. Sound financial planning; ensuring appropriate accountability of Trustees, staff and volunteers; implementing a clear policy and planning process; organising and minuting trustee meetings and annual general meetings; setting up agendas and preparing reports; ensuring proper safeguarding; and providing training for new volunteers—all this was putting a huge strain on the office with its limited resources.

This was significantly compounded by the discovery that much of Charles' work was literally 'locked up' on his computer and not readily accessible to the Trustees. In addition, Careers South West (CSW) suddenly announced they would be terminating Lucia's contract at the end of December 2018. County Council reorganisation, arising from the impact of austerity, meant that A&IT was facing another existential crisis.

The next trustees meeting was scheduled for Monday 22 October. This provided a few weeks for Julia to meet up with Lucia and the team in the office, the trustees, and a number of the members and volunteers. These opportunities were crucial in helping Julia assess the strengths and vulnerabilities of the charity. Most importantly, these conversations identified a deep, collective commitment to the cause and that the work of A&IT was making a real difference in people's lives, both volunteers and members.

Clearly, the loss of Charles had been profoundly unsettling for everyone, not least Lucia, who had worked so closely with him for six years. Chatting with her and learning more about the history of the A&IT journey enabled Julia to weigh up the significance of Lucia's role as Manager of A&IT and the implications of her growing involvement with the new Focus Frome hub.

The net result of these conversations, coupled with time to reflect and assess the next steps, provided Julia with an opportunity to open her first meeting as chair of trustees in October with a very clear, uncomfortably stark, proposition. 'Welcome to the meeting. We have two options before us—either we go for it or we shut down A&IT.'

Presenting the trustees immediately with such a direct statement was a bold but wise move. From the outset, no one present was under the illusion that the feel-good benefits arising for all involved in A&IT, and there were many, gave reason to turn a blind eye to the very serious challenges the group faced.

The assembled trustees were unanimous: 'We go for it.' All those present acknowledged the reality of the challenges and that a number of difficult decisions lay ahead, but the resolve was clear for all to see.

The purposeful and positive outcomes, from this first trustee meeting Julia had chaired, bore testimony to the fact that she was equipped for the role. From the outset, Julia invested her time and experience to address the foundational structure of A&IT whilst continuing to affirm and encourage all those on the front line. Quite simply, this enabled the work to continue. Her arrival could not have been more perfectly timed.

Shortly following that trustees meeting, I met Julia for the first time—under a table at Frome Town Football Club! A&IT were holding an afternoon Tea Dance on Remembrance Sunday and when I arrived a number of people had gathered rather anxiously around a table. Apparently one of the members, while dancing, had stumbled and grabbed an arm, pulling a man over. Clive had fallen under a table, headbutted the floor, and acquired a nasty cut on his head.

A nurse was needed and Julia, attending her first A&IT event as chair of trustees, had immediately got down to attend to Clive. Asked by Lucia, I also knelt to see whether Julia needed any help. In many ways it could not have been a better moment to meet Julia for the first time. I witnessed her using her experience to address the problem with calm, clear thinking and a comprehensive assessment of the situation. These qualities brought reassurance for all who were there, not least Clive, who remembers the moment well. Julia's experience benefited Clive on that occasion; it is that experience which A&IT also needed as it addressed its own challenges.

The succinct yet detailed six pages of the minutes from that first meeting of trustees, chaired by Julia in October, so clearly reveal the detailed and attentive way she immediately began to address the situation. Included in the minutes was confirmation that CSW had formerly written to say that Lucia would be made redundant on 31 December. This news served only to strengthen the resolve of the trustees, and an important decision was made to organise an away-day for staff and trustees in mid-November. The facilitator was to be Kate Hellard, Frome Town Council's 'Community Development Manager'.

The Town Council is committed to encouraging the role of volunteering in the community and the work of local charities; their support for A&IT, not least at this critical moment, has always been very highly valued. The Away Day focussed upon four key issues—vision, mission, values, and objectives. The gathering was very fruitful and served to bring real focus and purpose through the next, highly challenging months.

Some welcome encouragements

Inevitably some of the required changes in governance and procedures impacted rather uncomfortably upon the staff and the wider team, who were already unsettled by the loss of a dear friend and colleague. However, a commitment to the cause and the emergence of welcome new faces helped to hold all things together.

The arrival of two new volunteers Patricia and Peter Baker, residents of Frome and retired teachers, brought great encouragement, as do each of the volunteers who contribute in such a variety of creative, faithful ways. Peter was grateful for the opportunity to resume his guitar-playing in some of the group activities (he had previously played with local bands) alongside his befriending role; Patricia generously offered to take the minutes for the trustees meetings in addition to writing the monthly newsletters.

The appointment of new trustees to replace those retiring from the role provided further encouragement. Claire Newton, head of information management for Dorothy House where she has served for twenty years, joined the team. Claire has a significant contribution to make in the realm of implementing business requirements and organisational strategies. This might sound rather 'over the top' for a relatively small charity but the creation of a strategic business model brings untold freedom and benefits for all participants. Claire's quiet, thoughtful, and practical contributions have proved priceless through what has been and remains, albeit for different reasons, a very challenging period.

For some reason, my under-the-table 'moment' with Julia had prompted her to ask whether I would become a trustee. It was a privilege to become involved in this way with a group that has been close to my heart from its conception.

Carol, already relishing her role as a volunteer, made another valuable contribution. She decided to go the extra mile with an offer to oversee the presentation of financial reports for the trustees. It was an offer very gratefully received.

Nothing Is Permanent except Change

In February 2019 Becky Rhodes, who had offered sterling work in the office for a few hours each week, had the opportunity to move to a new job. Since she had joined the staff team, both Somerset You Can Do and VISTA had for financial reasons handed over their oversight and funding responsibilities to Careers South West. CSW is a much larger, more corporate body that seemed somewhat distant from the work being done in Frome, and one of their key requests was for much more statistical data. As well as regular details of the number of volunteers and beneficiaries, reasons for people joining and leaving the charity together with time and motion studies were regularly requested. Much of this landed upon Becky who dealt with a rather laborious role extremely efficiently.

The data bank, assiduously compiled by Becky, proved to be a valuable legacy, identifying priorities that needed to be addressed. Both CSW and Becky had 'left their mark'.

Development of the Focus Frome Hub

In the midst of all these procedural and personnel changes for A&IT, the Focus Frome Hub was beginning to establish its roots. Understandably this became evermore demanding for Lucia as she fulfilled her dual role as A&IT manager and practice manager for the emerging hub. Inevitably this raised the question about the viability of her continuing in her dual role.

It was a far from straightforward decision to make for all parties involved. Lucia had clearly played a key part in the birthing of A&IT and, having grown and nurtured the group for seven years with deep relational integrity, the thought of her leaving was difficult to countenance. Nevertheless, having harboured a calling in her heart since childhood to become a counsellor, the opportunity of entering the world of counselling with such a group as Focus, helping to build and shape the new hub in Frome was compelling. After much discussion (and not a few tears), the decision was made to release Lucia in September 2019, enabling her to pursue her work with Focus, and to advertise the post of service manager for A&IT.

Dougie

A number of people applied, three were interviewed and Dougie Brown, who had moved to Frome with his family in 2017, was appointed to commence the role on 1 August 2019. Following a career spanning many years as a senior army officer, he had spent six years working for the Prince's Trust as the operations lead for education, training, and development programmes. Given his experience and qualifications in strategic planning, leadership, and managing change, Dougie brought a skill set to A&IT which was extremely timely. As a recent arrival in Frome, he and his wife, Emily, wanted to engage with the grassroots of the community and the proposed role with A&IT perfectly served this purpose.

Through August Dougie shadowed Lucia, met with colleagues, took the opportunity to make a number of local connections and acquired a feel for A&IT's culture and rhythm of life. It was a fruitful month and ensured the transition worked as smoothly as possible.

As had been the case with Julia, Dougie's first month was challenging. Earlier in the year the charity's 2019 AGM had been scheduled for

Monday 16 September, which happened to be the anniversary of Charles Wood's death. It seemed so very appropriate that this would mark the moment when it was clear that A&IT would be continuing to pursue the path that he had played a key part in defining. Julia, his final interviewee and successor as chair of trustees, presented a report for the past year which clearly revealed the magnitude of the changes that had been undertaken.

Dougie then delivered his first manager's report; he had been in post for five weeks—in effect eleven working days as Julia pointed out. It was clear to all that he had grasped the values, background, opportunities and challenges underpinning the charity. He reported that A&IT had three part-time staff, including himself, 105 members, with a further 15 waiting to join, 71 volunteers and ten more awaiting DBS (Disclosure and Barring Service) confirmation. He estimated that within the year, there had been a total of almost 5,000 interactions and engagements arising from events and meetings. Following earlier discussions with trustees, staff, volunteers and members, Dougie outlined five key objectives: growth to more than 200 members by 2024; greater intergenerational emphasis; accurate reporting of events; clear sustainable financial governance and funding; and greater collaboration with other providers, particularly the NHS.

As 2019 drew to a close, there was a sense that a quiet order and purpose had been restored to A&IT following two years during which tales of the unexpected had shaped much of the headline news. Departures and significant changes in staffing; rebuilding the group of trustees; ongoing financial uncertainty compounded by county council decisions; the hovering shadow of austerity—each generated potential challenges. However, appointments had been made, decisions had been taken, and a collective commitment had been sustained. At last it was possible to imagine that A&IT was stepping into relatively still waters.

A decade was drawing to a close and the 2020s were about to arrive. A growing, palpable sense of anticipation filled the various Christmas and New Year A&IT celebrations.

What glad tidings would New Year 2020 bring?

CHAPTER 5

Tales of the Unimaginable: 2020

> The object of a New Year is not that we should
> have a new year. It is that we should have a new soul.
> —G. K. Chesterton

> Never let a good crisis go to waste.
> —Sir Winston Churchill, 1942

> The only thing worse than being blind is having
> sight but no vision.
> —Helen Keller

A New Year and a New Decade Beckon

Stepping into a New Year with all the associated parties, fireworks, and celebrations has never truly resonated with me. I'm more of a morning person and find it almost impossible to stay awake until midnight, even on New Year's Eve.

Making New Year resolutions has never been a high priority either. I only begin to think intentionally about the coming year when potentially life-changing events have already been written in my new diary. Such entries have included the dates of university finals, holidays, my wedding day, and the anticipated birth of a daughter or son. Each New Year in question promised significant moments and stirred me to seriously ponder some resolutions. These were rather more deeply embedded than the usual crop of ideas which are invariably cast aside by the end of January.

New Year resolutions, however lightly or seriously we take them, seldom settle for more of the same. Rather, a deeper purpose lies behind them as we ask ourselves what might I do or stop doing in the coming year(s) to reshape my life and become more fully alive. Hence the arrival of a New Year, irrespective of how we celebrate it, serves as a prod, gentle or otherwise, to wake up to the fresh opportunities before us. We need those prods because the reality is that, to some degree, we each sleepwalk through much of life. Henry David Thoreau, an American philosopher, once stated, 'To be awake is to be alive. I have never yet met a man who was quite awake.'

It is, of course, a truism that not one of us is *fully* alive because this gift of life we possess, no matter how long we live with it, takes more than a lifetime to fully understand. Hence, in a quietly repetitive and persistent way, the annual re-arrival of the opportunity to make New Year's resolutions invites us to reflect upon our path in life. The arrival of every New Year subtly re-presents two personal questions:

1. Why am I here?
2. What is the purpose of my life?

Curiously however, notwithstanding all I have said above about my distancing from all the annual New Year hype, I actually *did* find stepping into AD 2020 significantly different. I concluded this was for one reason and the clue is to be found in the very number '2020'. But why the fascination with 2020?

Throughout our lives, the number 20/20 has been associated with our vision. What we 'see', our perspective on life, matters—yes, *really* matters. As I prepared to step into 2020 I found myself pondering how might my vision be sharpened in the coming months. If the year *did* change my perspective on life, what would be the defining moments that caused the change(s)? The answer would prove to be beyond my wildest imagination.

The association of the term 20/20 with vision was established over 150 years ago with the birth of the familiar eye chart. We've all faced these charts as we've undergone eye tests, screwing up our eyes as they progressively moved from top (easy) to bottom (almost impossible).

The growing impact of the industrial revolution through the eighteenth and nineteenth centuries had led to an explosion of mechanisation. This demanded a greater dexterity amongst the workforce and, in many realms of work, good sight. To meet this demand, a significant step forward was made by the Dutch eye doctor Herman Snellen, Professor of Ophthalmology at Utrecht University. He responded in 1862 with his design of the familiar Snellen chart which universally standardised the measurement of sharpness of vision. This eye chart rapidly became the global standard for eye tests, remaining so until the twenty-first century.

The normal Snellen chart has eight lines of block letters. The person being tested stands 20 feet away, covers one eye and reads out the letters in each row, starting from the top. The row containing the smallest letters we can read identifies the acuity (sharpness) of that specific eye. The fourth row up from the bottom measures what the 'normal' human being can read from 20 feet and this is described as 20/20 vision. If we have 20/30 vision, we can only read from 20 feet what normal sight would read from 30 feet. The usual requirement for holding a driving licence is at least 20/40 vision, and the threshold for legal blindness is 20/200. The top letter on the Snellen chart is one which normal vision would recognise from 200 feet, whilst a blind person would need to be within 20 feet.

The value of good eyesight and the desire for vision correction have been acknowledged by humanity for many centuries. What we see really *does* matter and Helen Keller's quote reminds us that what we see is much more than simply a mechanistic, physical matter. In addition to the five senses—namely sight, hearing, taste, smell, and touch, each deeply valued—we also possess intuitive senses. These ancient tools, all too often unrecognised, collectively bestow upon each of us a capacity for awareness. The term coming to our senses literally means fully waking up to what *is*. All of us, to some degree, need to come to our senses as we continue to sleepwalk through many realms of life.

Helen Keller's personal story is fascinating. Born in 1880, at the age of nineteen months she contracted an unknown illness which left her deaf and blind. Mark Twain, reflecting upon her life declared, 'The two most interesting characters of the 19th century are Napoleon and Helen Keller.' Through the encouragement of her teacher and companion Anne Sullivan, who accompanied Helen for nearly fifty years, Helen was the first deaf/blind person to graduate with a BA degree in 1904, and she went on to become a leading suffragette, pacifist, radical socialist, author, and worldwide speaker.

Few people would be in a better position than Helen Keller to declare, 'The only thing worse than being blind is someone who has sight but no vision.' Helen recognised that our natural senses, such as sight and taste, only partially perceive the 'world of appearance'. It is our intuitive senses through which we perceive those deeper layers of existence, occasionally referred to as the 'world of essence'. This view of the world, which embraces more than a purely mechanistic p

is essential if we are to understand our experience of and r

the living world we inhabit. In short, we need both sight *and* vision, for as the ancient text reminds us, 'Where there is no vision the people perish.' (Proverbs 29:18).

What better year than 2020 could there possibly be to reflect upon our vision for the future, our perspective on life? It was this thought which had triggered my sense of anticipation for New Year 2020. With hindsight, irrespective of age and culture, 2020 confronted each and every one of us with one fundamental question: how will the journey through this year change my vision, my perspective on life?

Sir Winston Churchill, alluding to the devastation following the Blitz in the Second World War, declared, 'Never let a good crisis go to waste.' His choice of the words 'good crisis' initially sounds rather odd. However, the quote reminds us that whatever impact a crisis brings, no matter how uncomfortable, there are important lessons to be learnt and questions to be answered. Following a crisis, we should never simply endeavour to 'move on' as if nothing has happened.

We will each have our own memories from our encounters with Covid-19, experiences which will portray quite contrasting pictures, and our answers to the questions will be many and varied. Whatever they are, few would deny that the impact of the months which followed March 2020 was both terrifying *and* clarifying; this impact will continue to be profoundly significant and life-changing. Any dream of 'returning to normal' has been swept away and, as we return to life, a common experience will be similar to that of reverse culture shock. We discover we are returning to a place that is not quite as we had remembered it. This can be profoundly unsettling.

Yet, however unsettling it is to accept that the world, both locally and globally, has changed, it is important that we do not waste the journey we've all taken through 2020. Both personally and collectively, we need to humbly address the realities unveiled and to acknowledge the huge challenges presented. We need to be alert to the new opportunities beginning to open up.

The Arrival of the Unimaginable

Through the early weeks of 2020 the presence of the Covid-19 virus in the UK went largely unnoticed, although daily news bulletins reported its spread across the globe. The first confirmed UK victim of the disease was Peter Attwood, who died on 30 January. When the symptoms of the disease were more widely known and understood, several people (including my wife) recalled suffering the symptoms in February. With little medical information at that time, the symptoms were largely dismissed. The storm was gathering, but no one quite knew where it would lead; in the meantime, we all continued to get on with our business. For A&IT, there remained much to do.

Having recently started as service manager, Dougie spent his first six months getting to know colleagues, familiarising himself with the culture and working principles of A&IT, and learning more about the culture of Frome. His first AGM report had made clear the charity was busy clarifying a number of policies and procedures.

With helpful data continuing to be gathered, the regular weekly meetings held by the staff (all part-time, collectively working under forty-five hours), and trustee meetings being held every six weeks, real strides were made on many practical issues. Governance, clear policy statements regarding safeguarding (including the provision of DBS checks), health and safety, risk management, staff contracts, and induction for volunteers were each addressed. Two issues given particular attention were the introduction of a Phone Befriending Service and a clear financial strategy for the charity.

The potential benefit of providing a Phone Befriending Service was that it would provide greater flexibility for staff, members, and volunteers to communicate with one another throughout the week. With limited office working hours confined to Mondays and Tuesdays, the addition of this service would enable both staff and volunteers to operate much more freely in both time and space without necessarily having to travel further. By February 2020, phone-befriending volunteers had been recruited, training had been offered, and the benefits were soon clear for all to see.

A priority for all charities is to pay due attention to the provision and management of finance. Even though A&IT is relatively small in size, for many years it had received successive oversight and partial funding from county-based agencies, notably VISTA, 'Somerset You Can Do' and Careers South West. The decision by CSW to end their contract in December 2019, for financial reasons meant that, in order to continue operating, A&IT would have to become fully independent and provide its own funding. All evidence indicated the charity was growing, and the trustees acknowledged that costs for training, travel, hire of office and rooms for groups, delivery of service, and staff hours would inevitably rise. Much discussion ensued regarding the appointment of a fundraiser and Helen Sprawson-White, who had played a key role locally in fundraising, notably with the local cancer charity Why, was approached. Her task would be to develop the role of fundraising for A&IT and incorporate it with the organisation's use of social media.

The impact Helen had upon the charity's profile was immediate. Responses to Facebook, Twitter, and Instagram rose significantly and, together with articles in the *Frome Times*, the face of A&IT was becoming more widely known in the community. The important role of a fundraiser was confirmed and it became apparent that further hours would be needed to develop this role. Because of personal circumstances and demands upon her time in other work spheres, Helen felt she could not offer this but her contribution had made clear to everyone the vital importance of the fundraising role.

Trustee Alan Didymus had addressed fundraising in a dedicated way and, together with Dougie and other trustees, continued to work hard submitting bids for funds, a time-consuming business. A number of applications were fruitful, and this generated much encouragement and heartfelt thanksgiving. However, the perennial problem of securing financial security to enable the work of A&IT to continue remained.

A national survey in 2019 revealed one in five charities were struggling to survive financially, and the potential impact of Brexit upon the economy compounded the uncertainty. Within months, as Covid-19 began to appear on the scene, the chief executive of the National Council for Voluntary Organisations, Karl Wilding, stated, 'Charities are under pressure like never before. Smaller, locally-based charities are especially exposed to the crisis.'

Understandably the trustees and the staff team continue to be hugely relieved and *deeply* thankful for each and every grant received. However, for some time many had felt uncomfortable that the majority of our funding came from distant sources. We were, in effect, competing with other charities facing their own needs. In the light of this, it was becoming increasingly apparent that the ideal way of securing financial security for A&IT was through local community fundraising. A prerequisite for this to happen was the need to continue to increase our local profile, gaining trust and understanding from all those with whom the charity engage.

It is no exaggeration to say that addressing all these tasks in the months following the 2019 AGM proved to be very demanding, not least for Julia, Dougie, Di, and Gwen who were also accommodating a growing number of much-welcomed members and volunteers. Not for the first time in the short history of A&IT, the timing of the significant steps being taken proved to be unimaginably serendipitous, a reality revealed as February drew to a close.

From March 2020, it had become very apparent that Covid-19 was well and truly in charge of events and running the world ragged. Daily announcements were made introducing fresh closures, restrictions, and cancellations until finally, on 26 March, the Health Protection Regulations which itemised sweeping restrictions became legally enforceable. Within days, the daily UK Covid-19 death toll was mounting by more than 100 a day.

Inevitably the rapid introduction, multiplication, and consequences of the lockdown measures had an immediate, significant impact upon everyone, including every strand of A&IT. All group meetings were stopped on 16 March, and one-to-one befriending ceased on 23 March. Both were immediately replaced by one-to-one phone calls, both for group members and befrienders. Within a few weeks of being set up, the Phone Befriending Service was certainly proving its worth.

It was profoundly encouraging that social media requests to the wider community throughout January and February had brought a significant number of new volunteers on board. The 71 listed at the AGM had grown to 155. Equipped with a current DBS, a brief phone guidance document and a seven-slide safeguarding Power Point, it remained possible for them to engage with the ever-increasing number of members, which had risen from 105 to 179 in the previous six months.

Further benefits from the Phone Befriending Service came from unexpected sources. A daughter living in Singapore was very worried about her mum in Frome, who was shielding and isolated. The daughter had heard about A&IT on Facebook and got in touch with the office, which was able to set up her mum with one-to-one befriender phone calls. When lockdown measures eased, the befriender continued her shopping role and began visiting.

On another occasion, an elderly man in his eighties was seen shopping in ASDA when he should have been isolating. When asked why he was taking the risk, he said he had to get his food on his own as he was not online and didn't even have a phone. When this news was conveyed to the ASDA Frome 'Community Champion' and A&IT Trustee, Jackie Bryant, she contacted the A&IT office which sent out a request for any old phones, bringing a quick response. A 99 pence SIM card (incoming calls only) was purchased, the gentleman was given the phone and, every Tuesday morning thereafter, he would receive a phone call from the office for a chat and his shopping list which was later delivered to his flat. This was possible because of the links which had grown between A&IT and Shop for You, a project established at the beginning of lockdown by the town council.

The added value of phone-befriending had been immediate. One associated story illustrates the important part improvisation plays when we address the unexpected. One of the members was profoundly deaf and the deep sense of loneliness and isolation, generated by repeated lockdowns, was proving particularly difficult. In response, her befriender became a pen pal, exchanging notes on a regular basis and, when it was permissible, joined a 'support bubble' in order to renew visiting. The limitations imposed by lockdown measures served to create another pathway. Where there's a will, there's a way!

There were periods in the summer when groups, maintaining social distancing, were able to meet outside. A long-time faithful and insightful volunteer Ruth Suter, one of the first trustees, had engaged with the Tuesday Group meetings for some time and deeply missed the regular camaraderie. She suggested the group relocated to Victoria Park when weather permitted, and her endeavours played a key role in sustaining the momentum for this group. The year culminated in an excellent gathering in Victoria Park to celebrate the Christmas Festival, with music delivered on the stage by Peter Baker and shared mulled wine. One of the benefits of this regular, socially distanced gathering continuing through 2020 was that new members and volunteers were briefly able to meet up with the wider group. In so doing they could capture a 'taste' of how A&IT operated in a communal, relational context – a principle which lies at the heart of the charity.

It was at one of these gatherings in the park that I met one of the new volunteers, Georgina Richards, a recent newcomer into the Frome community and a research student in the Faculty of Humanities at Bath University. Geors has over fourteen years of experience managing projects and programmes in community development sectors in the UK and developing countries. Currently, she is evaluating the Bath and North East Somerset Compassionate Communities project and, having moved to Frome, she discovered A&IT and joined the growing team of volunteers. Geors relished the prospect of being a participant in befriending Frome rather than simply observing from an academic perspective.

This proved to be a gift to both A&IT and Geors. For her, the experience served to both affirm and deepen her understanding of the way in which volunteering plays such a key role in social welfare and brings political and social change. Not least, it cultivates a strong sense of belonging to both place and society. In addition, meeting up with both members and volunteers confirmed the findings of academic research which declared that volunteering should not be seen as a unidirectional activity but as beneficial for both parties. From the beginning, A&IT has been a non-hierarchical group intentionally aiming to work *with* rather than *for* others. 'By the forming of networks and the creation of a movement where all stakeholders come together, it's possible for everyone to win. Working *with* establishes momentum and empowers all participants.'[1]

For A&IT, it has been so helpful having Geors' grassroots perspective on the work of the charity. Having asked the Trustees whether she could have a chat with both volunteers and members, a brief note was circulated through one of Patricia's monthly newsletters. If they wished, members and volunteers were invited to get in touch with Geors and share their experiences and assessment of A&IT; all names were omitted, and no confidences were breached. It was a very welcome exercise both for Geors with regard to the dissertation she was writing and, importantly, also for the trustees given that the past two years had witnessed so many unexpected changes and challenges.

It was inevitable that, however hard people worked, some matters would be overlooked and mistakes made. The introduction of social distancing meant that Di and Gwen were severely restricted in the opportunities they had to meet up with volunteers and members to get to know their interests and challenges. This is a vital step as they endeavour to ensure the befriending pairings are mutually beneficial. It is this relational work that most engages Di's and Gwen's hearts. As Di reflects,

> The thing we enjoy most is interacting with members and volunteers, visiting people who have made a connection with us, getting to know them a little bit and matching them to the correct volunteer who has similar interests. This is something we have sorely missed over the pandemic when we can only phone new contacts and cannot interact as much as normal. Seeing or hearing from our members who have been so happy

with the volunteers they have been given, who have made such a difference to their lives, is our greatest joy.

While the summer months of 2020 saw the lifting of some lockdown restrictions, permitting the resumption of a few group activities, A&IT endeavoured to sustain its response to wider developments. When lockdown measures were imposed at the end of March, Frome Town Council established and funded the Shop for You project. With much of the town council's work restricted, they redeployed two staff to organise and run the project, collecting shopping for those who were shielding and confined to their homes. By the autumn, those staff were needed to return to their familiar council roles, and Frome Town Council wanted to hand over the work to A&IT as the philosophy and rationale of the two groups was very similar. Although funding remained uncertain, the opportunity to work *with* the group felt right to the trustees. Further discussion led to this being put into practice towards the end of the year, with Shop for You and A&IT working in a partnership and benefiting all parties.

Interviews also took place to appoint a paid fundraiser to succeed Helen and it was a joy to appoint one of the volunteers, Tracey Rawlins. Tracey had worked for nearly thirty years in Arts Marketing and Venue Management, including time spent fundraising for the Cheese and Grain; she is also a professional photographer. Securing this appointment as the anniversary year approached was a significant and very welcome step.

At the same time, another local group was pondering its next steps, Frome Community Drivers. FCD was the brainchild of Frome Town Council, which in 2017 had placed an advert for a project coordinator in the *Frome Times*. This was spotted by Richard Fry who had recently retired having spent a lifetime serving in the army before overseeing the administration of a road haulage company in Shepton Mallet. A local resident in Frome for many years, Richard was looking for an opportunity to serve the community and the town council were delighted to appoint him to lead FCD. The group engaged the assistance of Sustainable Frome and Mendip Drivers for a period and Richard explored the possibility of linking up with A&IT. However, at a time when the financing and future of A&IT were far from certain, the idea wasn't then viable.

In 2019, Morag Stuart was appointed to succeed Richard and lead FCD, which grew steadily and purposely. Having received a legacy gift in appreciation of the project, Morag began to weigh up the possibilities of either setting up her own charity or working in collaboration with another charity. Given the befriending role of A&IT and the associated need for transport to take members to groups and events, it was clear the two charities had much in common. In the autumn, it was agreed to explore the idea once again, and the merger was accomplished by the end of 2020. A few months later, Richard Fry was asked whether he would agree to join A&IT's board of trustees. This was quickly agreed by both parties.

The year 2020 drew to a close with A&IT having reached more than 250 members and engaging more than 210 volunteers. It is little surprise the five-year strategy Dougie had presented at the September 2019 AGM, with the objective of reaching 200 members by 2024, had been blown out of the water by the arrival and ongoing redefining presence of Covid-19. Looking back upon the year, it was remarkable to record the number of occasions when a successful finance bid, the arrival of a new volunteer, the addition of a new member, or a fresh idea from someone came at just the right moment. A willingness amongst everybody—members, volunteers, staff, trustees, and those offering support, such as the town council—to go above and beyond what had been promised, anticipated or requested was both humbling and inspiring. This served to generate a growing resolve in everyone involved.

2020 had been so full of the unexpected—or, more realistically, the unimaginable—and this was significant for A&IT as it was preparing to mark its tenth anniversary in 2021. Plans for this had begun to be drawn up in the summer of 2020, acknowledging that all plans would be provisional given the unpredictable consequences of Covid-19. Three priorities emerged:

1. Celebrate with the wider community the positive and speedy response to the many and various challenges the pandemic had presented.
2. Focus on ensuring financial stability to ensure A&IT could plan for the future.
3. Clarify the A&IT vision for the next decade in the light of lessons learnt from the past ten years.

As the chimes rang out to mark New Year 2021, the UK faced at least a further ten weeks of confining lockdown measures. Stepping into the New Year, life continued in the community and A&IT with few celebrations and little discernible change.

In effect, further lockdown delayed the marking of the New Year until mid-March, when the first tentative steps which were due to be taken by the government to begin to ease the restrictions on daily life. The glimmer of light this offered to A&IT was the promise of an opportunity to recommence outdoor gatherings in Victoria Park on Tuesday mornings, albeit with social distancing and masks.

Could this mark the possibility of new beginnings?

1. *Incarnational Ministry: Being with the Church* (Norwich: Canterbury Press, 2017), p. 9.

CHAPTER 6

Tales of Emerging Hope: January – March 2021

> We may have all come on different ships, but we're in the same boat now.
>
> —Martin Luther King

> It is the quality of our relationships that, more than anything else, determines our happiness, fulfilment and the sense of a life well lived.
>
> —Sir Jonathan Sacks

> Coronavirus and social distancing forced all of us to look loneliness in the eye.
>
> —Oliver Dowden, MP

> Volunteering is a well-hidden jewel whose social worth is rarely the subject of public valuation.
>
> —Andrew Haldane

A Difficult Present and an Uncertain Future

Every New Year celebration is inextricably linked with hope but the arrival of 2021 brought muted celebrations; for weeks, there had been daily news reports of rising numbers of Covid-19 victims in hospital and a sobering daily death rate. New variants of the virus had emerged and there was little immediate hope of easing lockdown restrictions. As a result, a sense of fragility was everywhere and hope felt strangely rationed at the very moment it was so sorely needed. Of all New Year beginnings in recent decades, few, if any, were in greater need of hope. Hope, as we know, is an essential ingredient if we are to live purposeful lives when faced with not only a difficult present but also an uncertain future.

For many, perhaps the most familiar and engaging signs of hope in the new year are those we witness at our feet—notably the arrival of snowdrops and early daffodils. These symbols seem strangely apt, serving as a reminder that so often hope arises from the grassroots of the natural world, sometimes from the smallest seed. The value and positive impact hope can impart to human life is widely recognised. It can be deeply transformative, personally and communally, not least because it can be so easily shared.

The image of a rainbow has been used by many cultures over millennia as arguably the most powerful symbol of hope. Initially associated with the story of Noah's ark in the opening pages of the Bible (Genesis 9:12-17), the rainbow is a memorable, universal symbol of God's covenant (promise) to establish an enduring, unending relationship of commitment with all creation, through all generations. Clinical psychologist Charles Snyder comments, 'Just as the sight of a rainbow can lift our spirits, hope can been described as "a personal rainbow of the mind."' (1) It is perhaps little wonder that the rainbow was inextricably associated with the public's heartfelt gratitude in response to the herculean efforts of all NHS staff throughout the Covid-19 pandemic.

Through the early months of 2021 (I write this in May), A&IT received a number of totally unexpected rainbows of the mind and each served to cultivate an enduring hope during the dismal, dark days of the ongoing pandemic. Month by month our spirits were lifted at opportune moments.

January: Rainbows of the Mind

For A&IT, hope flowed from the grassroots decisions and actions taken in previous months. The link with Frome Community Drivers, organised by Morag Stuart, was up and running in time to assist vulnerable and isolated people to get to the vaccination centres. Meanwhile, Shop for You was continuing to grow at a steady rate as vulnerable individuals were increasingly being asked to isolate.

In addition, a befriending project, Shepton Together, was taking root in Shepton Mallet with Di and Gwen offering set-up support for branding and practice. Each of these developments generated hope for all parties involved and reflected the desire of A&IT members to share their endeavours, foster trust and collaboration, and remain responsive to the ongoing challenges.

On 21 January, the *Frome Times* announced the breaking news that A&IT had been chosen as Frome's *Group of the Year for* 2020. The newspaper invites members of the community to nominate candidates for this annual award and a panel of local representatives select the winner. The reason this accolade generated so much delight and hope in the ranks, at the onset of the tenth anniversary year, was not least because it was a decision made by the whole Frome community.

People had written such encouraging comments with their

nominations, including one that stated, 'This charity does wonderful work every year, but in 2020 they were a lifeline to so many people in Frome and the surrounding community.' The award was humbling and all associated with A&IT are profoundly grateful to those who had voted.

The timing could not have been better, given that one of the key anniversary initiatives was to prioritise funding from local sources rather than relying upon distant and rather impersonal funding bodies. It is strongly believed that local funding serves to generate a deeper sense of community ownership, a mentality that in turn strengthens community cohesion and fosters a corporate feeling of belonging.

Having taken up her fundraising role at the beginning of the month, Tracey Rawlins immediately engaged with the emerging anniversary plans and her local knowledge and dynamic nature infected everyone with renewed enthusiasm.

One of the many surprises to be found in Frome is that it lays claim to over 350 listed buildings, more than any other town (including Bath) in Somerset. Wall plaques are everywhere, and this prompted an idea for the anniversary year.

In the autumn of 2020, A&IT began working with a local company, Compugraphic to discuss the design for wall plaques, exhibiting the charity's logo, which could be displayed on the walls, doors or in windows of homes, shops, schools, churches, and businesses. Anyone contributing £1 a week would be entitled to display a plaque, and their very visible presence around the locality would signal the collective community response being taken to look loneliness in the eye. (Oliver Dowden)

By the end of January, the A3, A4, and A5 plaques had been completed, together with coasters and car stickers. These are intended to be handed out in linen shopping bags stamped with the A&IT

logo, together with a little chocolate contributed by ASDA through Jackie Bryant, their Community Champion. The bags were provided, at no cost, by James Garven, a Frome resident and senior director of the Warminster-based Paper Bag Company. Distribution was planned to begin with the easing of lockdown measures. It is little wonder that such generosity, coupled with the design and production skills of Compugraphic, triggered further rainbows of the mind.

The prospect of bags, plaques, coasters, and car stickers being seen around Frome was eagerly anticipated. A simple calculation concluded that one thousand plaques, visible across Frome and the wider community, would generate sufficient funding to significantly sustain the work of A&IT, reducing reliance upon national funding bodies.

In this way, the community would be investing in its own wellbeing, and all generations could play their part. In a family of four for example, each week a different member of the family could contribute £1 from their salary/pocket money/savings. In this way, everyone, from the youngest to the oldest, would understand the importance of sharing what we have with others and discover the difference this can make to *all*.

January came to an end as lockdown continued. Gatherings were prohibited, news bulletins continued to deliver a litany of gloom, and weather forecasts promised cold, wet days. For A&IT, big steps had been taken, hope was sustained, but the present remained difficult and the future—as for everyone—uncertain.

February: Further Rainbows of the Mind

There is common agreement that February is the worst month of the year. Days are short and dark, a reprieve from winter is still weeks away and most, if not all, January resolutions have been laid aside. Perhaps we can be thankful that whoever invented February had our best interests at heart in making it the shortest month of the year!

Any glimmer of promise is welcome through these days—the glimpse of a yellow Brimstone butterfly, bearing the promise of spring, often does it for me. In the event, for A&IT the shortest month was not short of encouragement. The momentum continued to grow.

Having immediately prioritised the anniversary plans, Tracey organised the A&IT Valentine Raffle for a luxury Valentine's Day hamper, the contents of which were very generously donated by the local business community. A wonderful response raised almost £600, and it was a joy that the winner was Suzi Mitchell who has been a precious volunteer since 2013. In addition a local stonemason, Stephen Barker, set himself the challenge of completing 500 km on his rowing machine over the course of one hundred days as part of his personal keep-fit campaign. Stephen identified A&IT as his favoured charity on Local Giving and successfully completed his challenge. Well done and a huge thank you, Stephen, and to all who contributed to A&IT through similar ventures. It was truly humbling to receive such support.

The trustees and staff reflected how best to begin distributing the plaques, initially to those who had already pledged support in the business and commercial realms. Frome Railway Station was identified as an ideal location, not least because a plaque would be one of the first things visitors arriving by train would set their eyes upon.

Designed by T. R. Hannaford, an assistant to Brunel, the station opened on 7 October 1850 and is one of the oldest through-train-shed railway stations in the UK. A grade 2 listed property, the station has long had a heritage plaque and, because of its historical significance, we needed to receive permission from Great Western Railway (GWR) to to place a plaque. An email was dispatched on Sunday evening, 7 February, outlining our purpose, vision and values and the role of the plaques.

GWR instantly grasped both the significance of the purpose of A&IT and our desire to attract local funding. The impact of the pandemic upon the railways has been huge, and they had reflected on the strategic changes they would need to make in response. Their overriding conclusion had been that they had to prioritise support for local communities and participate in their recovery. In 2020, unbeknown to us, GWR had concluded one of the most important elements in their contribution would be to address the problem of loneliness and isolation and to contribute towards rebuilding more cohesive communities (see Appendix for a copy of their excellent Community Cohesion Policy document). Their plan is to share this strategy with towns along with their network in Wiltshire, Somerset, Devon, and Cornwall.

Within days of receipt of the email and following a conversation over the phone, GWR immediately endorsed the model of A&IT and pledged their support. In particular, they agreed with the priority of focusing on local funding from within the community and, to underscore their support, they agreed to place an A3 plaque on the station *and* to cover the cost of producing all the plaques!

To describe this as merely another 'rainbow moment' scarcely does justice to the reaction; the possible outcomes from this connection with GWR are impossible to ascertain. It will certainly generate good publicity for Frome, and it will be glorious (not least for local businesses and local markets) to witness increasing numbers of curious visitors arriving at the station. The opportunity to welcome new faces to our streets and shops lies at the heart of rebuilding the fabric of community, deepening social cohesion.

In addition, opportunities will arise to share what is happening in Frome with other communities linked with the GWR rail network. This augments the work of Frome Town Council and has the potential to bring mutual benefits to both Frome and the other communities with whom A&IT engage. Generosity begets generosity; the benefits of shared purpose are to be widely spread.

Further confirmation of the priority to generate local funding arrived through a one-off grant from the Beatrice Laing Trust in London. The grant was accompanied by the following statement:

> We have now had an opportunity to consider your application for a grant to help finance initiatives designed to develop sustainable sources of local income as part of your 10th Anniversary 'celebrations'. The need to address loneliness and isolation across all generations has been highlighted by the Covid-19 pandemic and is an issue of which the Trustees of the Beatrice Laing Trust are acutely aware.
>
> They are however firmly of the view that, in order to be sustainable in the longer term, projects such as this must be funded primarily from local sources. They are, therefore, fully supportive of the steps you plan to take to raise awareness of your work and funding needs in the local community. Accordingly, I have pleasure in enclosing a cheque for £5000 as a one-off donation to help fund these initiatives.

To receive this donation *and endorsement of the expressed purpose of the tenth-anniversary programme* was deeply encouraging. In his recently published and acclaimed book *Supercommunities*, local author Keith Harrison-Broninski presents a powerful call for rebuilding society from the bottom up, bringing change from within to meet new challenges in times of crisis. The book highlights the key role that community ownership plays in enhancing a community, strengthening social cohesion, building community wealth, and growing well-being.

Published in February 2021, it includes an engaging account of the unfolding story of Frome, especially with reference to the significance of the past two decades. The book clearly affirms the truth that the story of A&IT is indeed 'a story within a story'.

At the end of February, a group of A&IT staff, trustees, and volunteers met united by the magic that is Zoom (quote in the monthly newsletter written by Patricia Baker). Most importantly this provided an opportunity for us to meet one another, albeit online, some for the first time after months of restrictions. The director of services (role renamed), Dougie Brown, shared encouraging news with regard to Frome Community Drivers, having been vaccinated to enable them to respond to increasing demand. Plans for resuming gatherings in Victoria Park, when permissible, were shared as was exciting news about the proposed Art Exhibition entitled *Portrayal of a Pandemic*, the brainchild of Co-ordinator Di Roberts.

February may be the shortest month, but it certainly delivered a number of 'rainbows', each generating further momentum and encouragement for all engaged with plans for the tenth anniversary of A&IT.

March Moments

Whilst we all eagerly anticipated the announcement of the earliest moment for recommencing group activities, it was encouraging to learn that the demands upon Frome Community Drivers in March had risen by over 60 per cent compared to the opening two months of 2021. Morag, who is at the helm, coordinates the journeys undertaken by her team of more than twenty-five drivers. Taking passengers for routine examinations and vaccination at Frome Medical Centre and Shepton Mallet Hospital certainly increased requests, alongside providing journeys to school for students with injury and mobility problems.

One of the drivers, Mervyn, is Frome born and bred. Having worked at printers Butler and Tanner for more than thirty-eight years before being made redundant, he became a driver for Mendip Community Transport and Dial-a-Ride. After a few years, Mervyn decided he wanted to do something for the community he has lived in and is delighted he took this decision to join FCD. Another driver, Debbie, moved to Frome from Sheffield two years ago and has been volunteering from the first lockdown. Having worked in a large NHS hospital, Debbie has always worked closely with people and wanted to get to know and to give something to the community in which she had now settled. Both Mervyn and Debbie love their role with FCD and, together with all the drivers, are very highly valued.

It is always encouraging when one of our volunteers is recognised for the contribution they make to the wider community. This month it was volunteer Radek who was recognised as one of the 'inspirational heroes' honoured with a *Civic Award* by the Town Council for his numerous volunteering roles, including the past three years with A&IT. He also supports the Frome Carnival Committee, Fair Frome, Frome Town FC (as Head of Security) and is an Ambassador for Frome Town Council, ensuring noticeboards are tidy and up-to-date. Radek lives in Westbury, is an inspiration to all and, together with all of us, had been waiting patiently for group activities to resume. Finally, to his and collective relief, the long-awaited moment finally arrived.

On Tuesday 30 March, the easing of lockdown enabled a group of A&IT members to gather in Victoria Park, some for the first time since March 2020. Social media had spread the news in the days leading up to the day, and it was such a joy to see members, volunteers, trustees and staff registering their delight at meeting up again. Arriving about half an hour after the appointed time, I was thrilled to see small clusters of people scattered around the bandstand and to hear Peter Baker's guitar and songs playing in the background. In spite of the social distancing, it was a joy to wander from group to group, to listen to the shared delight immediately generated following many months of lockdown. It was particularly encouraging that a wide spectrum of members and volunteers had gathered, both those who had recently connected with the group and those who had been involved with A&IT almost from the beginning. Reunions were made, newcomers were introduced to volunteers and members, and stories shared in quiet, relaxed conversations. It was a group which was being very 'active and in touch'!

In her monthly newsletter report, Patricia described the scene perfectly:

> Ruth, A&IT volunteer and the Tuesday Group Anchor, looked around happily, appreciating the lovely warm Spring day which had allowed people to come out and about. Helen, also a volunteer, declared she was so happy 'to feel connected with familiar faces again'. Rigorously observing the revised government guidelines of groups containing no more than six people, friends who had not met each other for months were able to talk and catch up … and what an event this proved to be.
>
> Member Clive shared the news that, using original sources and maps from AD 942–1515, he was researching into the Bounds of Mells and local place-names with a view to writing a piece for publication. Fleur, a recent volunteer supporting two members, was getting to know other volunteers, including Julie. Richard, an avid cricket fan, discussed England's latest

match with Peter as he enjoyed a cup of tea from the Café in the Park.

John, one of the group's oldest members at the age of ninety-five, was there. He first came to Frome in 1926 as a young boy to visit his grandfather, who had served in the navy in World War I. Following in his grandfather's footsteps, John was a merchant seaman in World War II who then settled in Frome. He was able to stay only for an hour however as, at noon, he needed to leave in order to help serving Meals on Wheels in the local area!

Eddie smiled as he looked round happily, describing how he used to come to the park every Tuesday and was pleased to be back. Member David, listening to the mellow music being played by volunteer Peter, was also delighted to be in the Park, seeing and meeting people. A former colour matcher at Weston Vinyls, he used to really enjoy making colours for new customers, and was delighted by nature's beautiful hues all around him. Another member, Marian, told Dougie Brown that following her letter from Matt Hancock, she had been sheltering and this was her first time out in ages. She had been brought to the Park by a Frome Community Drivers volunteer and was very much enjoying her surroundings in the very well-kept and manicured Victoria Park.

In many ways these encounters, and there were many more we could recount, portrayed the beating heart of the purpose of A&IT. The knowledge that at the first instance possible, following several months when some had never ventured outdoors, so many members seized the opportunity to gather again was a huge affirmation, confirming the value of what was taking place. As the GWR Community Cohesion statement declares,

Community cohesion lies at the heart of what makes a safe and strong community ... based on principles of trust and respect for local diversity, nurturing a sense of belonging and confidence in local people. (See Appendix).

Thus March2021 marks the completion of A&IT's opening decade. With days lengthening, wild flowers emerging, lockdowns easing, and holidays being contemplated the month drew to a close with a growing sense of public optimism. The time had arrived to celebrate the local charity's Tenth Anniversary.

[1] Charles R Snyder, 'Hope Theory: Rainbows in the Mind', *Psychological Inquiry (2002):* 249-275 at 269

CHAPTER 7

April 2021: An Astonishing Moment and The Abominable Mystery

> We are only as strong as we are united and as weak as we are divided.
>
> —J. K. Rowling

> Community is where humility and glory touch.
>
> —Henri Nouwen

> Never overestimate what you can do in one year; never underestimate what you can do in ten years.
>
> —Bill Gates

An anniversary affords the opportunity to express gratitude for all those who have helped to reach this milestone; an anniversary marks a time to pause and to clarify the vision for the future. As A&IT steps into its tenth anniversary, the world is beginning to emerge from 'the most disorientating, debilitating crisis most of us have ever known.' (1)

It is this global episode which requires us all to reflect, to re-evaluate and to reset; we cannot, as Churchill once stated, let a good crisis go to waste. Yet such a response calls for constructive dialogue and collaboration, humility and careful listening, each sadly a diminishing trait in society. How will this challenge facing society be 'heard'?

An Astonishing Moment on Easter Sunday, 4 April 2021

The nationwide closure of UK churches in 2020 was the first time for over 800 years that they had been closed across the nation - the previous occasion, coincidently, also being on 23 March in 1208. The Ecclesiastical Strike in 1208 was triggered by King John refusing to accept the Papal decision to appoint Stephen Langton as the Archbishop of Canterbury. Pope Innocent III responded by imposing an interdict, an ecclesial censure upon the Church, which lasted six years.

On the 23 March 2020, in response to government guidelines almost every church in the UK closed its doors but, before long, many churches gradually established online services. These have been greatly valued by those wanting to remain in touch with their faith community during the pandemic and, in many cases, the numbers attending online far exceeded the Sunday attendances hitherto.

On Easter Sunday 2021 my wife and I were following the online morning service at St Aldates Church in Oxford, a church with which we had had links in the past. In the middle of his sermon, the Revd Christopher Landau quoted these words which he had read the previous week in the *Guardian*:

> For many of us, life without God has turned out to be life without fellowship and shared meaning—and in the midst of the most disorientating, debilitating crisis most of us have ever known, that social tragedy cries out for action. (1)

Later that day I tracked down the article entitled *'How Do Faithless People Like Me Make Sense of This Past Year of Covid?'* It was one of the most honest, humble pieces of journalism I have read for a long time, opening with these words: 'Many of us yearn for meaning. But in our individualistic, secular society, we lack even the flimsiest of narratives to guide us.'

The author, John Harris, raises and reflects upon many questions - questions which we all harbour in our hearts but rarely discuss as we endeavour to make some sense of the times. It was only after further searching that I discovered John Harris lives - yes, in Frome, about 100yds away from our house.

Having recently filled in the 2021 census form, John describes how he and his partner both ticked the 'no faith' box and thought nothing of it. But then, for an hour or two, he felt a pang of envy as he wondered how religious believers were feeling in a year of lockdown with its fears and the sense of it all being random and senseless. He continues, 'Like millions of other faithless people, I have not the flimsiest of narratives to project on what has happened.'

Pondering this question, Harris had a long conversation with John Sabapathy, a medieval historian at University College London. The focus of their conversation focussed upon how Covid-19 compares to the Black Death and the ways societies and communities reacted to that disease in the fourteenth century. In conclusion, Sabapathy stated *the* most significant difference was that in the fourteenth century, 'those caught up in the plague did not cease thinking in terms of community and re-birth'.

Harris reflects that today a lack of social solidarity, arising from a mixture of individualism and collective denial, leaves many of us without the ideas or language to conceive of Covid-19 like that. Sabapathy adds, 'Perhaps the key contrast between the past and the present—and between people who still belong to religious communities and those who don't—lies in the 21st century's increasingly atomised world.' John Harris concludes his article with the rallying cry: 'That social tragedy now cries out for action.'

It was the reality of this 'social tragedy' that triggered the birth of *Hands at Work* in South Africa and, subsequently, A&IT in Frome. It is the current reality of this social tragedy that the past decade has unveiled, most notably through the lens of Covid-19. It is undeniable, as Harris argues, that *this* 'social tragedy now cries out for action' in a *sustained* way.

For centuries Frome has had a deeply embedded 'bridge mentality'. The bridge currently spanning the River Frome in the centre of town is the fourth bridge in that position, the original being built in 1667, and is one of only three in England (the others in Bath and Lincoln) with multi-storied shops built actually on the bridge. Now, in 2021, we need to keep alive that 'bridge mentality' for we are being called to build bridges of a different kind.

It is this calling that energises the Active and In Touch community as it marks its tenth anniversary in 2021. Together with the wider community of Frome, our desire is to build bridges in the wider community, calling forth deeper community cohesion. It's what Frome needs; it's what Frome does. *Frome: Made Differently*

The 'Abominable Mystery'

> The most beautiful thing we can experience is the mysterious, it is the source of all true art and science.
> —Albert Einstein

90

> Every mystery solved brings us closer to the
> threshold of a greater one.
>
> —Rachel Carson

Most of us find delight in discovering wildflowers, not least the bluebells in their prime at the end of April. It is such an encouragement, too, seeing members of the Frome community working collectively to protect local meadows and encouraging the planting of locally resourced wildflower seeds. Yet it is deeply distressing to acknowledge that the UK has seen the catastrophic destruction of once widespread wildflower meadows as intensive farming has gradually replaced them.

Experts say 97 per cent of the nation's meadows have been eradicated since the 1930s, which has contributed to the downward spiral of Britain's butterflies and bees. In the light of this, Rodden Meadow in the heart of the town is such a precious part of Frome. In the course of one year, more than 25 per cent of the fifty-nine UK butterfly species can be observed in the meadow (seventeen species were recorded in 2020).

Our love of wildflowers is because they are both beautiful *and* an essential part of our lives; flowers provide food for insects and animals and are the basis for many medicines. We love them, so why have we allowed 97 per cent of the nation's meadows to be eradicated in less than a century? It is a distressing statistic and disturbing question.

When he was a small boy aged seven years, Charles Darwin was depicted holding flowers in a pot. He, too, loved flowers and is best known for his contributions to the science of evolution. Towards the end of his life, Darwin was haunted by a big question. How did the first flowering plants appear on Earth so suddenly, relatively recently on the geological time scale, and then swiftly diversify in an explosion of colour, shape, and form? He was deeply bothered by how flowering plants conquered the world seemingly in the blink of an eye while other large groups, such as mammals, evolved gradually.

One of his problems arose from the fact that an essential element of natural selection in the theory of evolution is *Natura non facit saltum* (nature makes no leap). The sudden appearance in the fossil record of flowering plants and their rapid spread challenges this idea. Faced with this dilemma, Darwin coined the phrase 'abominable mystery'.

Fellow scientist William Carruthers, a Scottish botanist and keeper of the Botanical Department of the Natural History Museum at that time, was arguing for divine intervention (anathema to Darwin) to explain the fossil record. Unlike Darwin, Carruthers had no problem with the possibility of sudden, significant change. Whatever, despite their deep disagreement over the origin of their beloved flowers, both Darwin and Carruthers were united in their collective joy of flowers and readily continued to work and research together.

One hundred and forty years on, is the mystery solved? Responding to this question Richard Buggs, professor of evolutionary genomics at Queen Mary University of London, is in no doubt. 'No. Of course, we've made lots of progress in our understanding of evolution and in our knowledge of the fossil record, but this mystery is still there.' (2)

Living with mystery, whatever its frustrations, can bring deep meaning to life, and it is both sad and wrong that the binary question 'Do you believe in creation or evolution?' has for at least two generations been offered as a 'test of faith', implying that faith and science are irreconcilable. Both are precious gifts for the well-being of humanity as the work of the Faraday Institute for Science and Religion fully demonstrates.

What place does this information have in the story of A&IT? Well, think back to the early years of the story, and you will recall three names integral to the founding and development of the charity, namely Anna Brindle, Lucia Chadwick, and Charles Wood.

For Anna, the key moment in her life which served to plant a whim of an idea in her head was triggered by work she had been doing with the youth group at Holy Trinity Church, Frome. Meanwhile, Lucia decided to join A&IT 'not long after coming to faith, having prayed very earnestly to be guided in what I can do, because I so wanted to integrate my faith with purpose'. For both Anna and Lucia, faith is foundational to their quest for purpose in their lives and their connection with A&IT.

When Charles joined the Royal Air Force, he was required to provide his personal details. Arriving at the question regarding his faith he dutifully filled 'C of E' in the box and attended regular military services. However, he freely declared that for him, having trained as an engineer, he could not fathom the 'impossible possibility' of the resurrection and the presence of God ... although he admitted he couldn't stop thinking about it. Notwithstanding his wavering commitment to faith, Charles' commitment to A&IT, together with Anna's and Lucia's, was total. From the very beginning, he glimpsed the potential contribution the charity could make in building community cohesion,

> creating a society in which people from different ethnic, cultural and religious backgrounds can live and work together with a common purpose, in an atmosphere of mutual respect and understanding. (see appendix)

These have become embedded values for A&IT. Trustees, staff, members, and volunteers alike seek to model that diversity in an open-handed way that is mutually rewarding and enriching. Yes, mistakes are still made, omissions can occur but these can lead to significant moments in which important lessons are learnt.

So now to the big question. 'What *do* wildflowers and A&IT share in common?' Wherever we believe their origin lies, whether in the realm of the divine or not, their design and purpose is to bring joy and benefit to all who engage with them.

Faith or no faith, we can *all* potentially benefit as we work together for the greater good in an atmosphere of humility, mutual respect and understanding. If we are to live life undivided, an important 'bridge' to be established in every community is that which removes the pervasive sacred secular divide. Stifling life in almost every realm in our communities and our work-places, the 'great divide' awaits to be bridged.

1. John Harries, How do Faithless People Like Me Make Sense of This Past Year of Covid? *The Guardian* (28 March 2021)
2. Helen Briggs, New Light Shed on Charles Darwin's 'Abominable Mystery', *BBC News Science and Environment*, 23 January 2021

CHAPTER 8

Epilogue

> Hope is being able to see that there is light despite all of the darkness
>
> —Desmond Tutu

> Hope sees the invisible, feels the intangible, and achieves the impossible.
>
> —Helen Keller

> Learn from yesterday; live for today; hope for tomorrow.
>
> —Albert Einstein

A Puzzle

Using the following 11 letters—D, E, E, E, H, L, N, O, P, S, S—create two separate phrases (each phrase has two words and includes all the letters).

Phrase 1: H******* ***

Phrase 2: E****** ****

These two phrases, each with exactly the same elements, offer completely contrasting perspectives. In one sense, this puzzle illustrates the huge challenge western society faces in 2021. How are we going to organise/deploy/share our talents and resources in the future? For decades we have sleepwalked along an unsustainable pathway; 'bystander apathy' is endemic. The following quote from Sonya Renee Taylor encapsulates the place in which we find ourselves today:

> We will not go back to normal. Normal never was. Our pre-corona existence was not normal, other than we normalised greed, inequity, exhaustion, depletion, extraction, disconnection, confusion, rage, hoarding, hate and lack. We should not long to return, my friends. We are being given the opportunity to stitch a new garment, one that fits all of our humanity and nature. [1]

This season calls for innovative ways of doing things. This is not a political statement, it is a response to the realities we face, locally and globally; realities that are so often overlooked, denied and ignored. The truth is that change, enduring change, arises from the grassroots *within the community*. The invitation is for all of us to engage with this reality.

Change requires courage, imagination, and hope—three values that have served to shape A&IT through these first ten years. For each generation, for every one of us in all our diversity, what lies ahead is the invitation and opportunity to make 'a world of difference'. To put it very starkly, we each have but two choices before us:

Be *'inactive and touchy'* or be *'active and in touch'*.

Which will it be? Neither choice is prescriptive, one diminishes life, the other can bring life in all its fullness. Using exactly the same resources, namely our human gifts and the riches of creation, one choice leads to a 'hopeless end', the other to 'endless hope'.

Now is the moment to make that choice. Which is it to be?

1. (brenebrown.com/podcast, 16 September 2020)

APPENDIX

GWR Community Cohesion Policy Statement

Community cohesion lies at the heart of what makes a safe and strong community. It must be delivered locally through creating solid networks based on principles of trust and respect for local diversity and nurturing a sense of belonging and confidence in local people.

Community cohesion is critical to the quality of life of local people, and GWR's Community Cohesion Fund can help play an essential role in facilitating this by supporting and providing seed funding for small community charities, enterprises, and station adopters.

Embedding community cohesion principles throughout local life can bring about real change. Building cohesive communities brings huge benefits creating a society in which people from different ethnic, cultural and religious backgrounds can live and work together in an atmosphere of mutual respect and understanding.

Cohesive communities are communities that are better able to tackle common problems, provide mutual support, and work together for a positive future.

A cohesive community is one in which:

- there is a common vision and a sense of belonging for all;
- the diversity of people's different backgrounds and circumstances is appreciated and positively valued;

- those from different backgrounds have similar life opportunities;
- strong and positive relationships are developed between people from different backgrounds and circumstances in the workplace, in schools, and within neighbourhoods.

Since every location is unique in its demographic and social make-up, the meaning of community cohesion in your area will need to reflect an understanding of these local circumstances.

Whatever your local circumstances, building cohesion between communities is a necessary step towards improving people's quality of life and their opportunity to achieve their potential. Viewed from the outside, a cohesive community is one in which people will want to live and invest.

Active and
In Touch Frome

Established 2011

Helping to combat loneliness and
isolation in our community

www.activeandintouch.org

Active and In Touch Awards in 2021

Local - Regional - National

Frome Times' Group of the Year 2020

Somerset County Council Group Award medal

Queen's Award for Voluntary Service

**The Queen's Award
for Voluntary Service**

· THE MBE FOR VOLUNTEER GROUPS ·

ACKNOWLEDGEMENTS

Just as 'it takes a village to raise a child and a community to raise a person', it takes a community to write a book. This book is dedicated to the A&IT community, the volunteers, members and trustees, past and present, who have generously shared their thoughts and memories. It is also dedicated to the Frome Town Council, who have consistently encouraged pioneer projects and volunteering for the past decade.

I am deeply grateful to Gary Watt for his generous and insightful foreword, highlighting the damaging disorder arising from loneliness.

I am ever grateful to my wife, Chris, for her patience with my obsessive preoccupations and to all who offered their wisdom in editing and publishing the book, especially: Emma Tuck, local authors Gill Harry and John Payne, Patricia Baker, David Revell and the team at AuthorHouse. Any omissions and errors are all mine.

Thank you, Anna ... for having the courage to share 'a whim of an idea'
Thank you 'team A&IT' ... for buying into and sharing the vision
Thank you Frome community ... for awakening to the need
Thank you Lord ... for the mustard seed and so much more

All profits from the sale this book go to Active and In Touch Frome to support its work in the local community.

https://www.activeandintouch.org

Lightning Source UK Ltd.
Milton Keynes UK
UKHW011849231121
394446UK00001B/18